# Introduction

Catholic Children's Bible Stories is a timeless and classic collection of the best and most beloved stories from the Bible, designed to introduce your children to the beautiful teachings of the Catholic faith.

Each story is carefully written in a child-friendly, engaging, and rhythmic manner, making it a perfect introduction to the Bible for beginners. The stories are not just for teaching and entertainment but are also designed to impart lifelong lessons, fostering moral values and an understanding of the Catholic faith.

Regularly reading these Bible stories to your children will instill wisdom that stays with them for a lifetime, paving the way for a successful, prosperous, and happy life (Joshua 1:8).

Repetition of good habits and teachings is key to proper parenting and instruction. The Bible teaches that if you instruct your children, they will give you peace of mind and bring delight into your life (Proverbs 29:17). A well-instructed child will grow up to make their parents proud.

As you turn the pages with your child and cherish these beautiful stories, your precious child can begin to foster a love for the Holy Catholic Bible and its timeless teachings. You are also nurturing a deeper connection with your child as you spend time reading and bonding with them. Most importantly, you are helping your child develop a love for God.

Ideal for young readers, this collection is a must-have for any family seeking to lay a strong foundation in the Catholic faith. May these Catholic Children's Bible stories become a cherished part of your child's upbringing, inspiring and guiding them on their spiritual path and relationship with God.

**Why Bible Stories Are Important for Children**

In a world that's constantly changing and moving forward, one thing remains timeless—the power of capturing stories. For generations, the Bible has helped instill valuable lessons, morals, and a strong foundation of faith. The stories contained in The Bible holds powerful and enduring significance, making it a rich source of wisdom for developing minds.

Catholic Children's Bible Stories contains the most iconic and meaningful narratives from the Bible, perfectly written to captivate and engage children. Stories like the courage of David facing Goliath, the faith of Noah building the ark, and the wisdom of Solomon are included. These stories aren't just about imparting religious knowledge; they're about igniting a love for the Bible and God.

Each story is presented in a child-friendly, rhyming, poetic, and fun-to-read way. Catholic Children's Bible Stories is a basic beginner Bible for kids and does not include all the details found in the Bible. As children grow older, the details of each story and event can be filled in.

These stories offer the most precious gift a parent can give their child—a moral compass, faith, and wisdom to last a lifetime. You're helping to teach lasting lessons that will guide your child to a bright future. Which Bible story or stories will become your child's favorite?

**Reading Together for a Stronger Bond**

Reading these stories with your child is not just about entertainment and instruction;
it's a very effective and important parenting method to strengthen the parent-child bond. It's an opportunity to create shared experiences, spark conversations, and provide guidance in a nurturing, loving, and fun way.

**Create an Enjoyable Reading Experience**

Here are some tips to ensure that both you and your child get the most benefit from these Bible stories:

**Select the Right Time**

Find a quiet, comfortable time to read with your child when you can truly focus and engage with the story together.

**Encourage Questions**

Be very open to your child's questions. Encourage them to ask about the characters, events, meanings, and lessons of the stories. This fosters curiosity and deepens their understanding.

**Make it Interactive**

Encourage your child to participate in the reading. Let them repeat words and sentences, and give them a chance to predict what might happen next. This makes the experience interactive and fun.

**Relate to Everyday Life**

Connect the stories to real-life situations. Discuss how the lessons learned from the Bible can apply to your child's life.

**The Creation Of The World**

In the very beginning, when all was dark and bare, God, the Creator, began to craft something special with great love and care.

On the first day, God said, "Let there be light." He named the light "day," and the darkness "night."

On the second day, with artistic flair, God painted the sky blue. Above and below, he split the waters from the sky.

On the third day, God separated the waters from the dry land. He called the land "earth," and the waters "seas."

On the fourth day, God set the sun, moon, and stars, causing them to light up the sky. The sun ruled the day with its warm golden light, while the moon's white glow graced the peaceful night.

On the fifth day, God filled the seas with all kinds of fish. In the skies, colorful birds took flight.

On the sixth day, God created more animals, unique in each way. From insects small to beasts so grand, He formed them all with a loving hand.

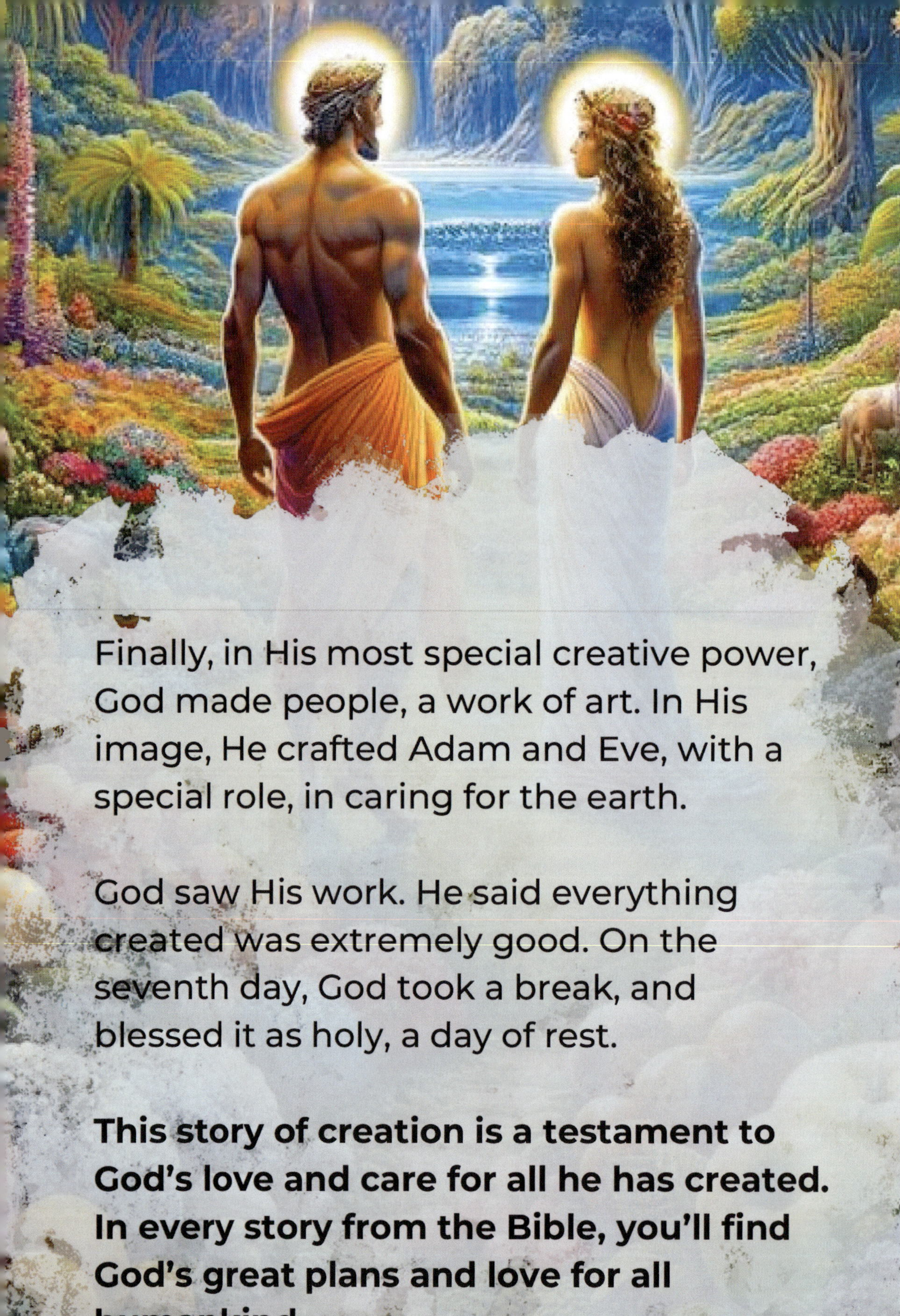

Finally, in His most special creative power, God made people, a work of art. In His image, He crafted Adam and Eve, with a special role, in caring for the earth.

God saw His work. He said everything created was extremely good. On the seventh day, God took a break, and blessed it as holy, a day of rest.

**This story of creation is a testament to God's love and care for all he has created. In every story from the Bible, you'll find God's great plans and love for all humankind.**

## Adam and Eve

In a beautiful paradise garden filled with all kinds of flowers, fruit, and animals lived Adam and Eve.

Adam and Eve, a perfect and happy couple, enjoyed their home in the paradise called Eden.

God had only one rule, “Don’t eat the fruit from the tree of life.”

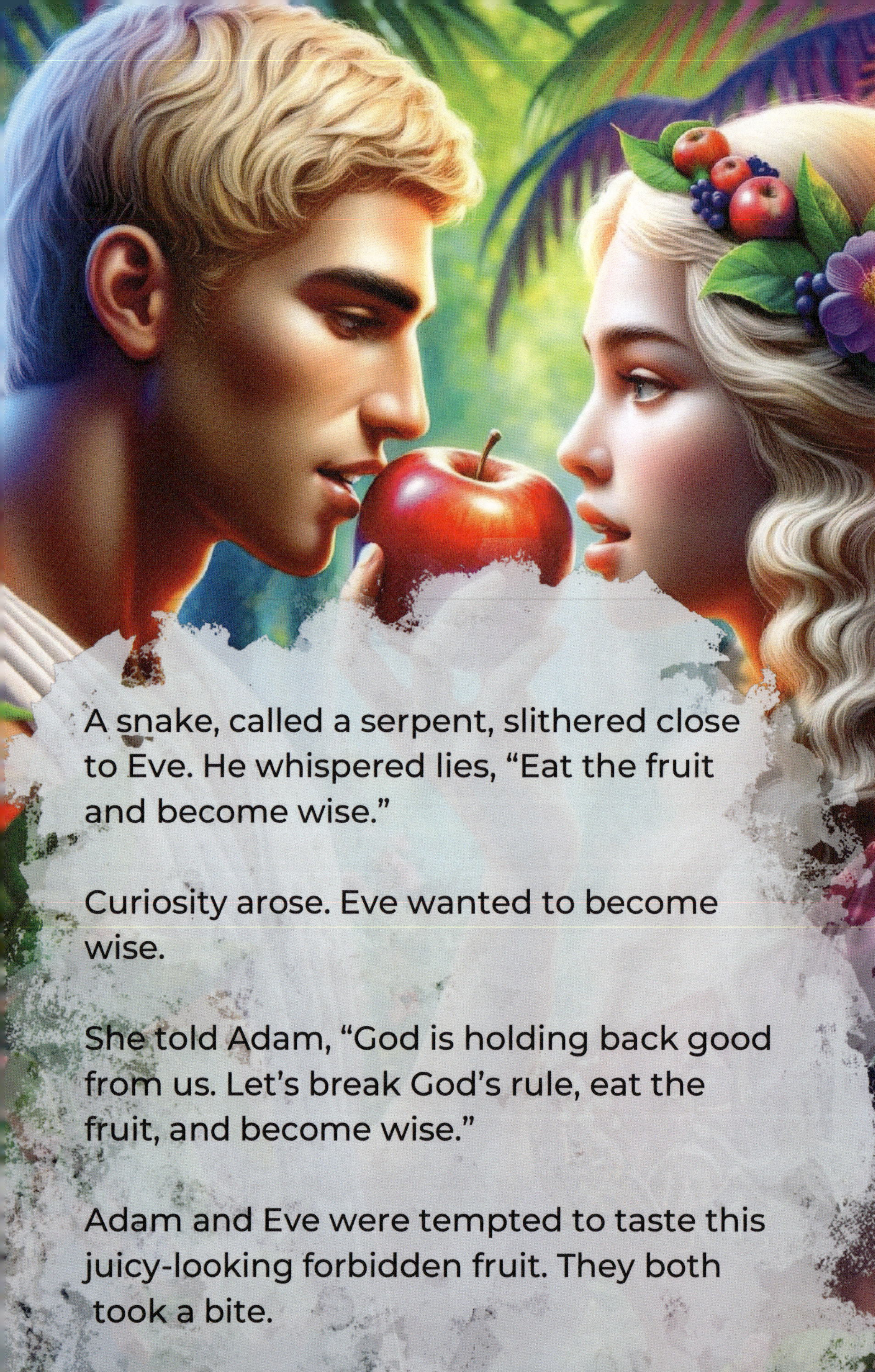

A snake, called a serpent, slithered close to Eve. He whispered lies, “Eat the fruit and become wise.”

Curiosity arose. Eve wanted to become wise.

She told Adam, “God is holding back good from us. Let’s break God’s rule, eat the fruit, and become wise.”

Adam and Eve were tempted to taste this juicy-looking forbidden fruit. They both took a bite.

God's voice echoed, "What have you done?" Adam and Eve suddenly became aware they were without clothes.

God provided them with clothes.

They left their home, Eden, with broken hearts.

**The story of Adam and Eve teaches the importance of obedience to God's rules.**

## Noah and the Ark

A long time ago, God gave a man called Noah an important task. He said, “Noah, build a large ship called an ark; a flood is coming to wash away the bad people of the land.”

Noah and his sons worked hard to build the ark. They gathered the animals, big and small, two of each kind, and food for all.

When the rain began to fall, Noah and his family hid safely away. Into the ark, they went, as water flooded the earth.

The ark floated high, like a floating zoo, keeping everyone inside safe as the waters grew.

Days turned to weeks, but the rain finally ceased. The ark found rest on Mount Ararat. Noah sent a dove to check for dry land.

Noah, his family, and all the animals stepped off the ark onto dry land. They thanked God, so happy to be led by God's care.

**Noah's bravery, trust, and hard work in building an ark teaches that you can navigate safely and find your way through the troubles and storms of life when you have faith and listen to God.**

## Abraham and the Promise

In the city of Ur, lived a man named Abraham and his wife Sarah, always trusted and listened to God.

One day, God spoke to him in a voice so clear: "Abraham, my friend, look up at the sky, count the stars you see. Your descendants will be as numerous as these.I promise you great blessings, trust in my word, for I have a plan.

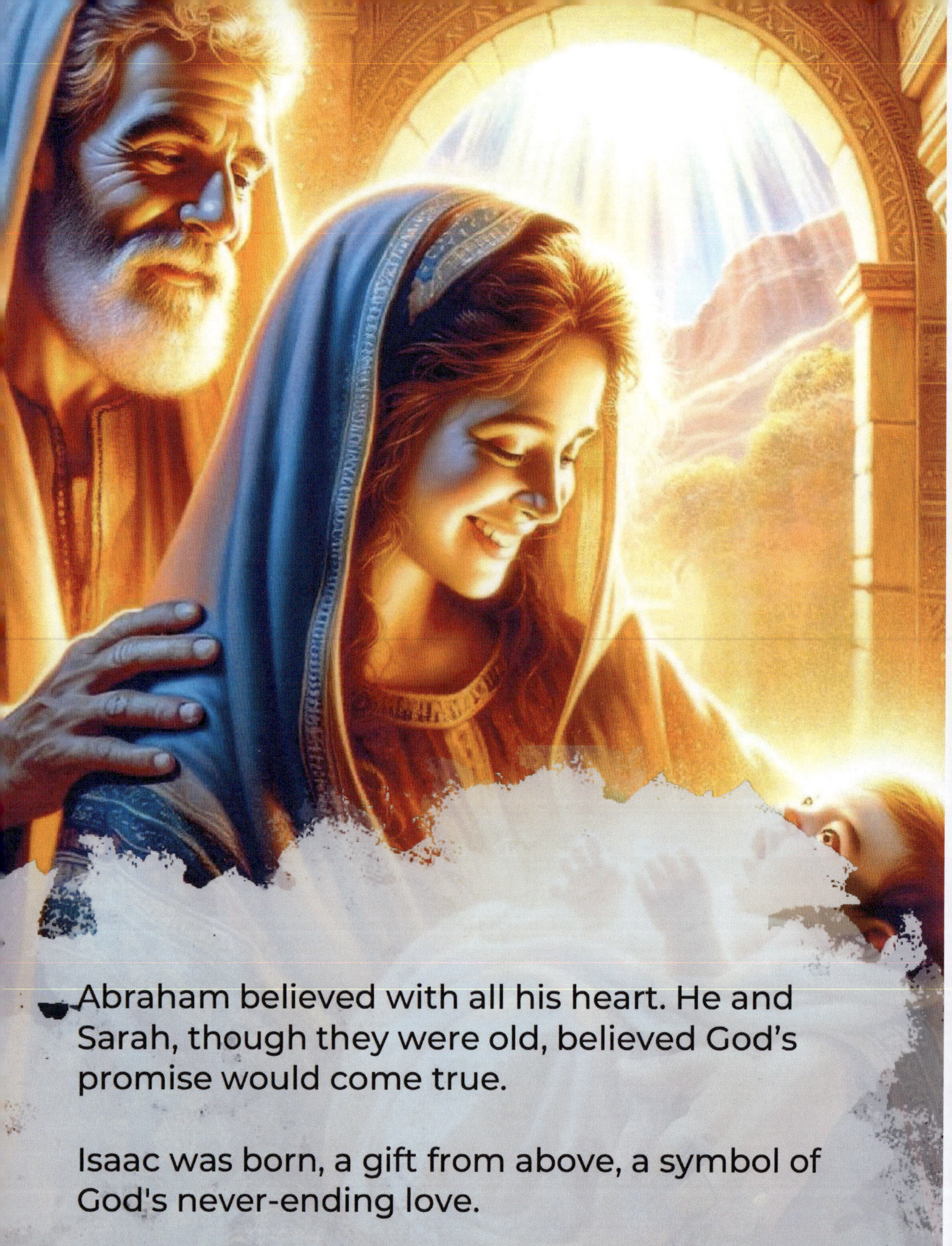

Abraham believed with all his heart. He and Sarah, though they were old, believed God's promise would come true.

Isaac was born, a gift from above, a symbol of God's never-ending love.

**With faith in your hearts, there's nothing to fear. Just like Abraham, trust in God's timing; His promises are guaranteed!**

## Joseph and His Colorful Coat

Long ago, in the land of Egypt, lived a boy named Joseph. His coat, a rainbow of bright colors, made him stand out in the sun.

Joseph received messages from God in dreams, of stars, the moon, and skies so bright—a future rise to power, his family bowing down to him.

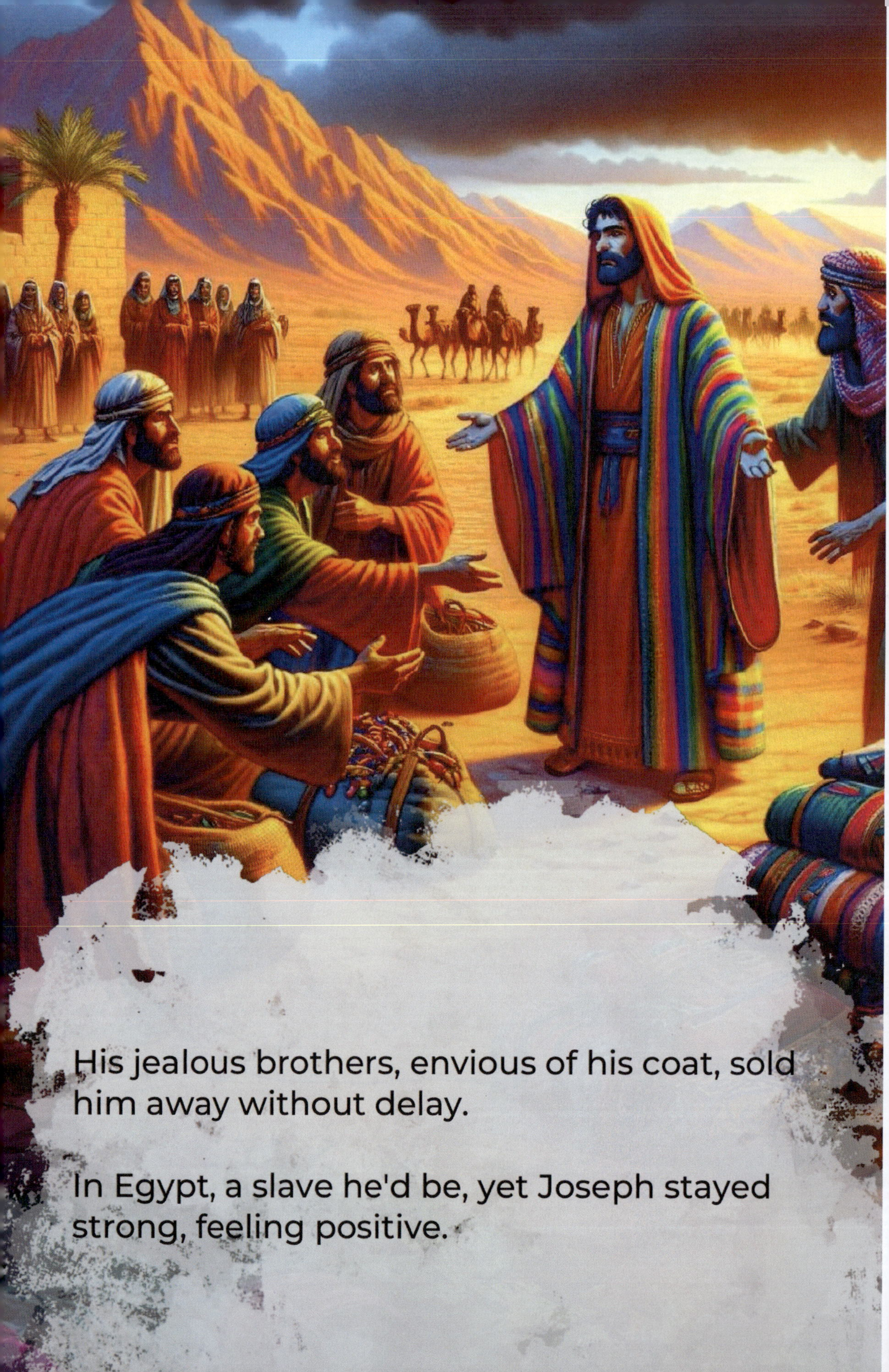

His jealous brothers, envious of his coat, sold him away without delay.

In Egypt, a slave he'd be, yet Joseph stayed strong, feeling positive.

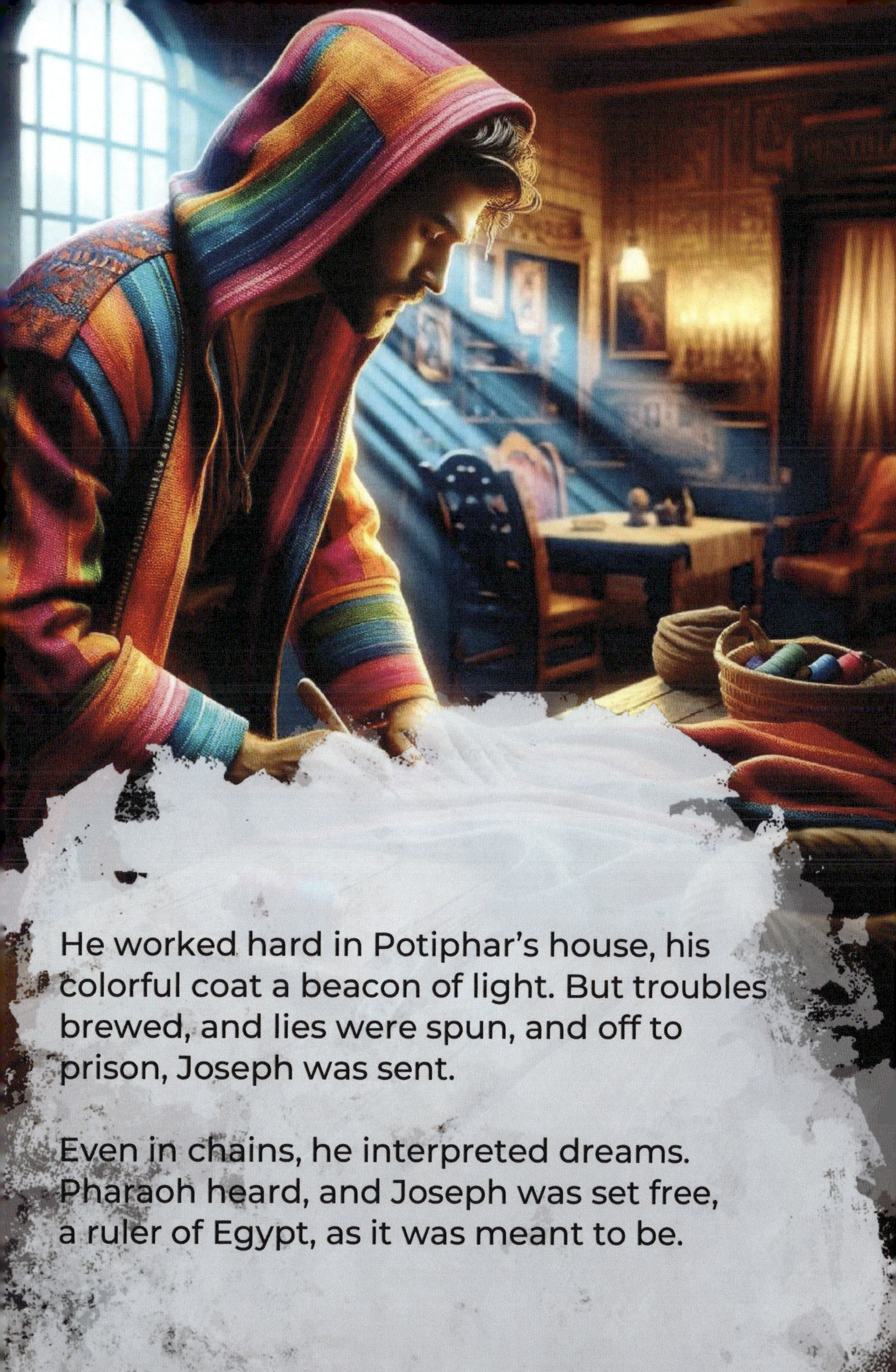

He worked hard in Potiphar's house, his colorful coat a beacon of light. But troubles brewed, and lies were spun, and off to prison, Joseph was sent.

Even in chains, he interpreted dreams. Pharaoh heard, and Joseph was set free, a ruler of Egypt, as it was meant to be.

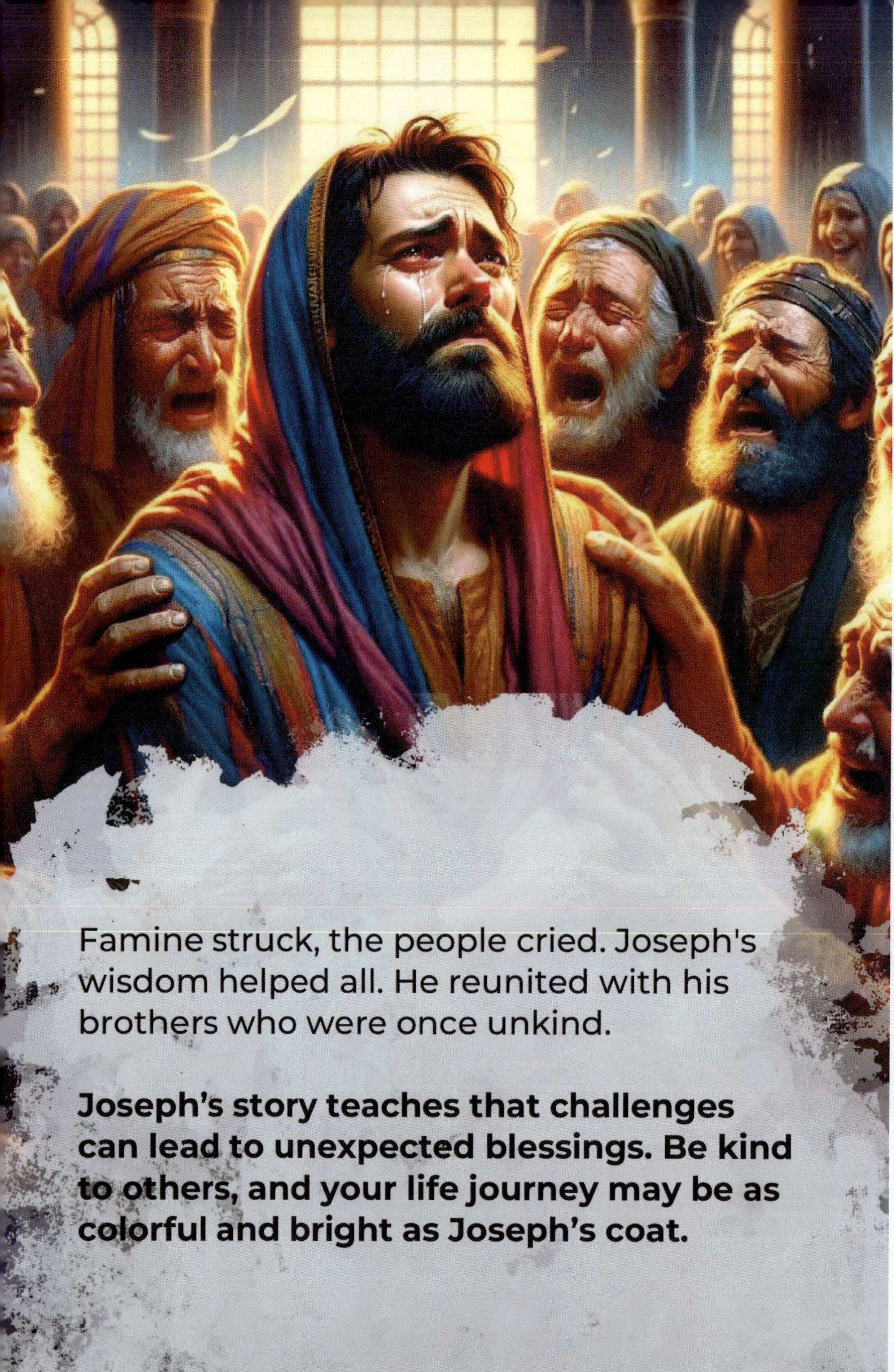

Famine struck, the people cried. Joseph's wisdom helped all. He reunited with his brothers who were once unkind.

**Joseph's story teaches that challenges can lead to unexpected blessings. Be kind to others, and your life journey may be as colorful and bright as Joseph's coat.**

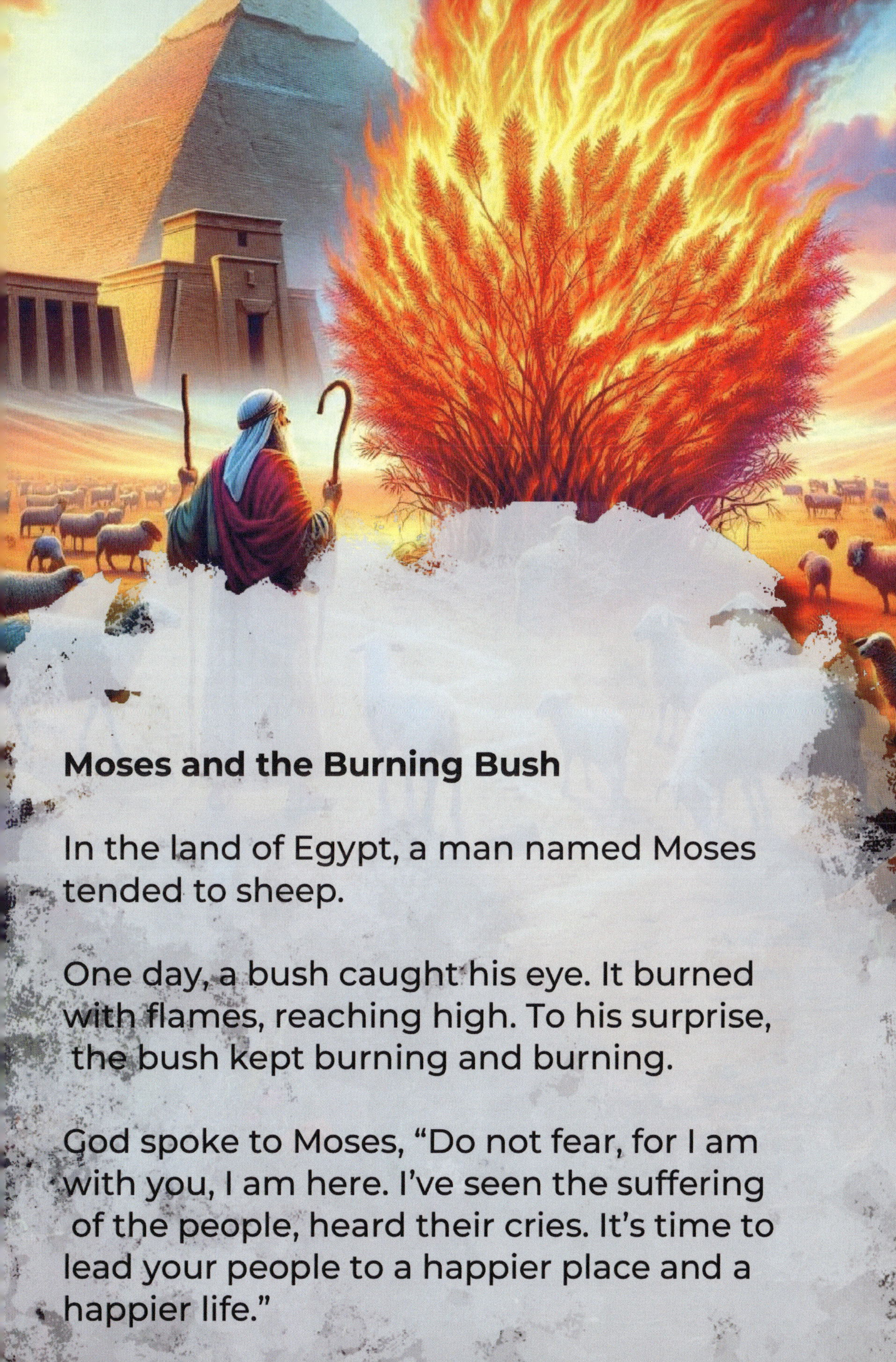

**Moses and the Burning Bush**

In the land of Egypt, a man named Moses tended to sheep.

One day, a bush caught his eye. It burned with flames, reaching high. To his surprise, the bush kept burning and burning.

God spoke to Moses, “Do not fear, for I am with you, I am here. I’ve seen the suffering of the people, heard their cries. It’s time to lead your people to a happier place and a happier life.”

The burning bush was a sight so magical and bright, a powerful sign on the darkest night. Moses understood that God could do powerful and amazing things, and he listened to what God told him to do it.

With staff in hand and a heart so trusting and bold, he'd lead his people, set them free, through desert sands and the mighty sea. Moses and God, hand in hand, led the way to the Promised Land.

**When life presents its challenges, like Moses, do not worry; you can find your way. Trust in God's love and guidance every day.**

## The Ten Commandments

Long ago, on a grand mountain, Moses climbed, guided by God's hand.

God gave Moses the Ten Commandments, a guide for life.

"Love the Lord," the first command.

"No idols," the second command.

"Respect My name," the third command.

The fourth command, truly blessed, "Keep the Sabbath, a day of rest."

"Honor your parents," the fifth command, and you will receive a long life and happiness.

"Do not harm others," the sixth command, life is precious, treat people with kindness.

“Be loyal when you get married,” the seventh command, love is precious, keep it special and sacred between two people.

“Do not steal,” the eighth command, respect other people and their belongings.

“Do not lie,” the ninth command, tell the truth to everyone you know.

The tenth and last command from God, “Do not covet,” be happy and thankful for what you’ve got.

**The ten commands are a guide to life, to help you succeed in life. Follow these commands, and you can be happy and blessed in life.**

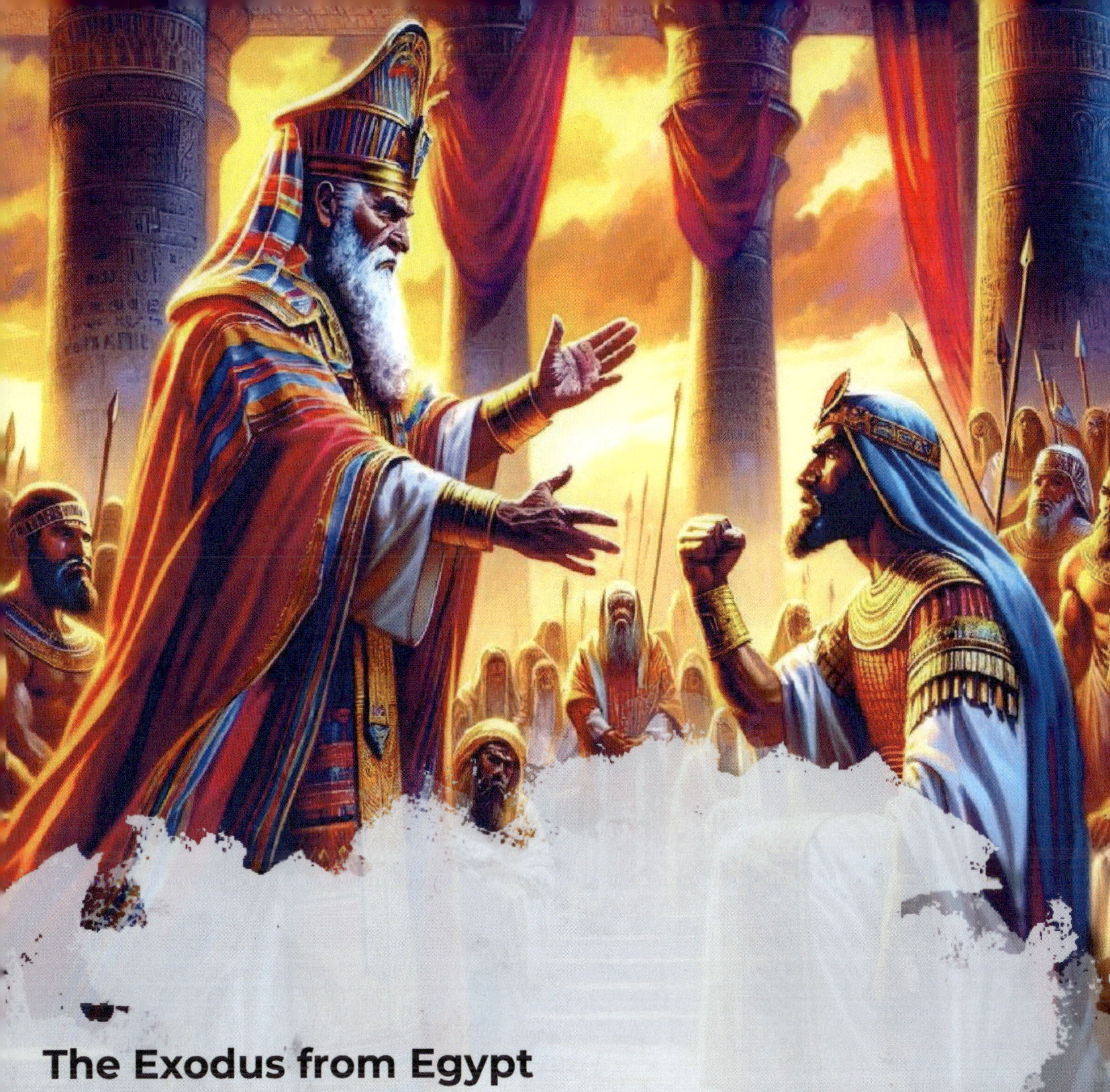

## The Exodus from Egypt

In Egypt, Pharaoh, the king, his heart was hard. God's people wanted to leave.

Moses asked Pharaoh, "Let my people go!" He told God's people, "It's time to go to a promised land!"

Pharaoh was stubborn, his heart was cold, so God sent ten plagues to help his people get free.

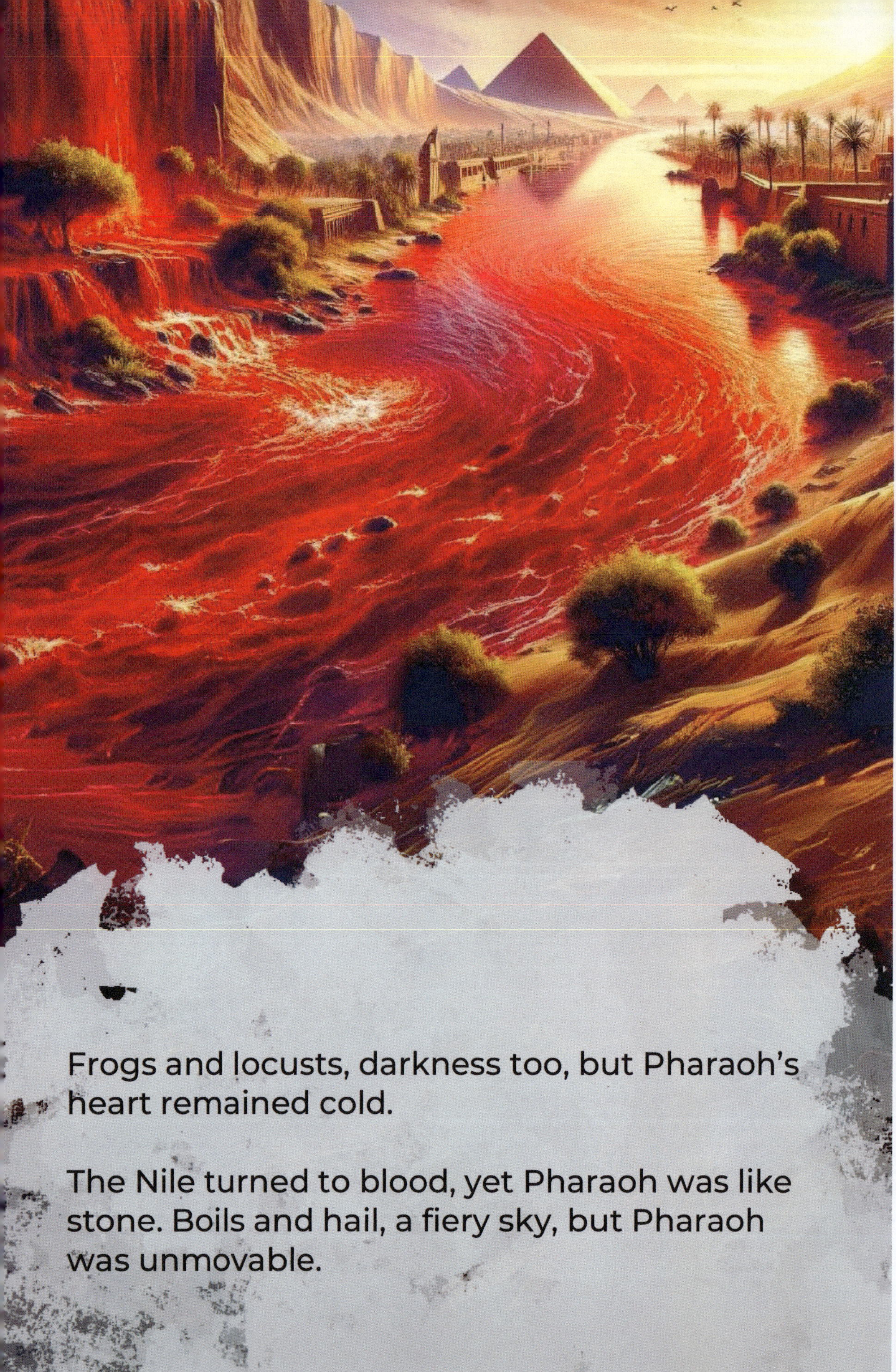

Frogs and locusts, darkness too, but Pharaoh's heart remained cold.

The Nile turned to blood, yet Pharaoh was like stone. Boils and hail, a fiery sky, but Pharaoh was unmovable.

The last and tenth plague, all firstborns were taken by God. Pharaoh was frightened, his heart softened. He said, "Go, leave, take your people with you!"

**The story of the Exodus from Egypt teaches about the power of persistence and the importance of listening to God. Faith and determination lead to blessings.**

## The Parting of the Red Sea

In the vast desert, God's people wandered. Their journey was tough, and they were feeling low. Pharaoh's heart, once again, turned cold. He came chasing after them with chariots.

Moses raised his staff up high, and God heard his prayer from the sky. The Red Sea parted—a miraculous sight. A dry walking path emerged right across the sea to dry land.

The people walked on dry, firm ground, with walls of sea water on each side of them. Chariots chased them from behind.

As God's people and Moses reached the dry land, the sea closed in, waves like a tide. The sea crashed down on Pharaoh's army, and God's people celebrated.

The Parting of the Red Sea teaches us that even when faced with impossible situations, God
can make a way for you. Trust in God's guidance, believe in miracles, and you'll find a path through any big challenge.

**The Fiery Furnace**

In the ancient kingdom of Babylon lived
three friends: Shadrach, Meshach, and
Abednego—strong and bold.

A giant statue, the king did create.
"Everyone bow down," was his stern dictate.
The three friends replied, "We worship God;
Him we'll never deny."

Into a burning hot furnace, they were thrown—a furnace so hot that everything melted before it even touched the flame!

Unharmed by the heat, the three friends, an angel from God shining so bright, danced with them in the fire—unharmed by the flames, what a magical sight!

**The story of Shadrach, Meshach, and Abednego teaches you to be strong and brave and know you can face any scary situation with God on your side.**

**Daniel in the Lion's Den**

Long ago, in Babylon, lived a man named Daniel—humble in every way. Kind and faithful, every single day, he knelt to pray.

The king in Babylon had a rule, that no one could pray to God but only to him. Daniel remained loyal to God instead.

The king grew mad. He threw Daniel into a den where the lions lay.

An angel from God came to Daniel to say, "Do not fear, for God is with you this day. The lions won't harm you, and you'll be okay."

It was a miracle. The lions lay still. The king was amazed. Faith in God kept Daniel safe.

**The story of Daniel and the Lions teaches that even when things seem scary, God can keep you safe. God is always with you and protects you.**

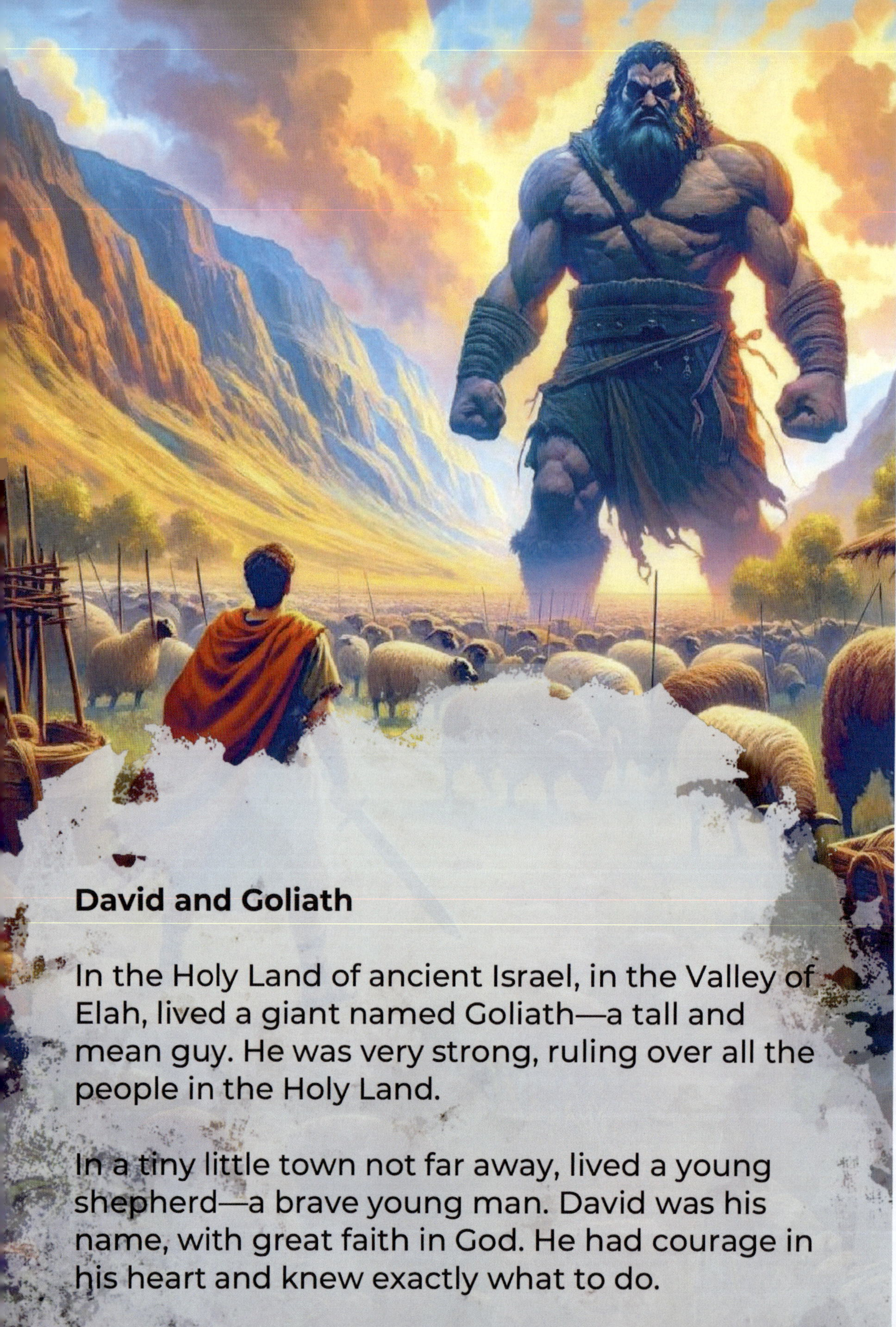

**David and Goliath**

In the Holy Land of ancient Israel, in the Valley of Elah, lived a giant named Goliath—a tall and mean guy. He was very strong, ruling over all the people in the Holy Land.

In a tiny little town not far away, lived a young shepherd—a brave young man. David was his name, with great faith in God. He had courage in his heart and knew exactly what to do.

One day, David was confident and ready. He stepped forward to confront the giant, with a sling in hand and a bunch of stones. Goliath growled, but David stood tall without fear, looking up at him. With God by his side, he knew he'd win.

He aimed his sling and let it fly. The stone struck up, up to the sky. The stone struck Goliath, and he roared. Down he fell—the giant was no more.

**In your life's journey, even when you feel small, do your best. With faith, courage, and God's guidance, you can conquer giants—your biggest fears—and win!**

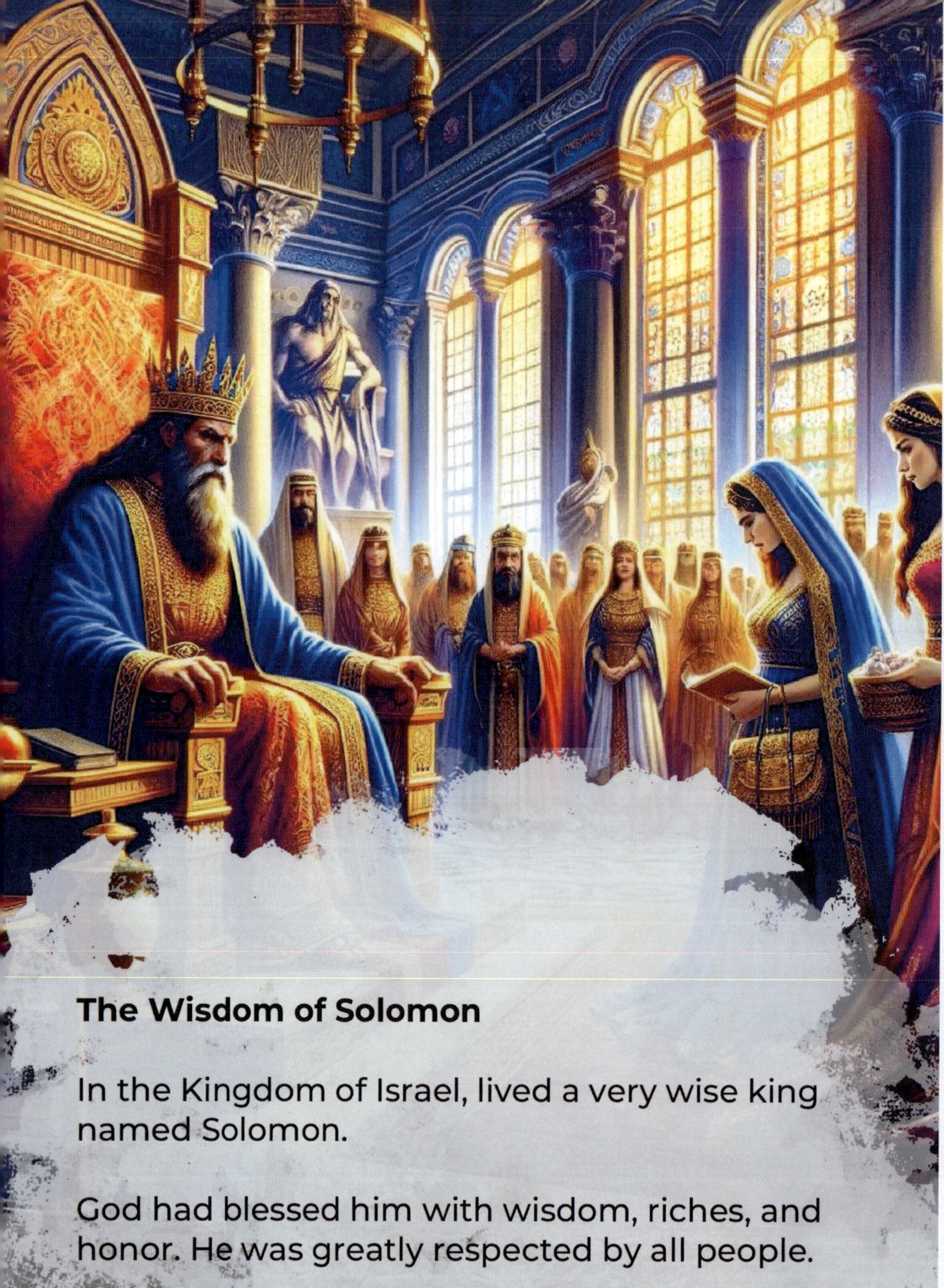

**The Wisdom of Solomon**

In the Kingdom of Israel, lived a very wise king named Solomon.

God had blessed him with wisdom, riches, and honor. He was greatly respected by all people.

Two women came to him, each claiming a child, both saying, “He's mine!”

King Solomon smiled. He knew how to discover the real mom.

“Let’s cut the baby in two!” he said. One woman agreed, the other one stared.

The real mom cried, “No! Spare my child’s life!” Her love revealed the truth; she refused to have her child cut in two. King Solomon declared, “She’s the real mom with great love for her child!”

**Ask God for wisdom when making important decisions. God will give you wisdom and help guide you when tough choices are to be made.**

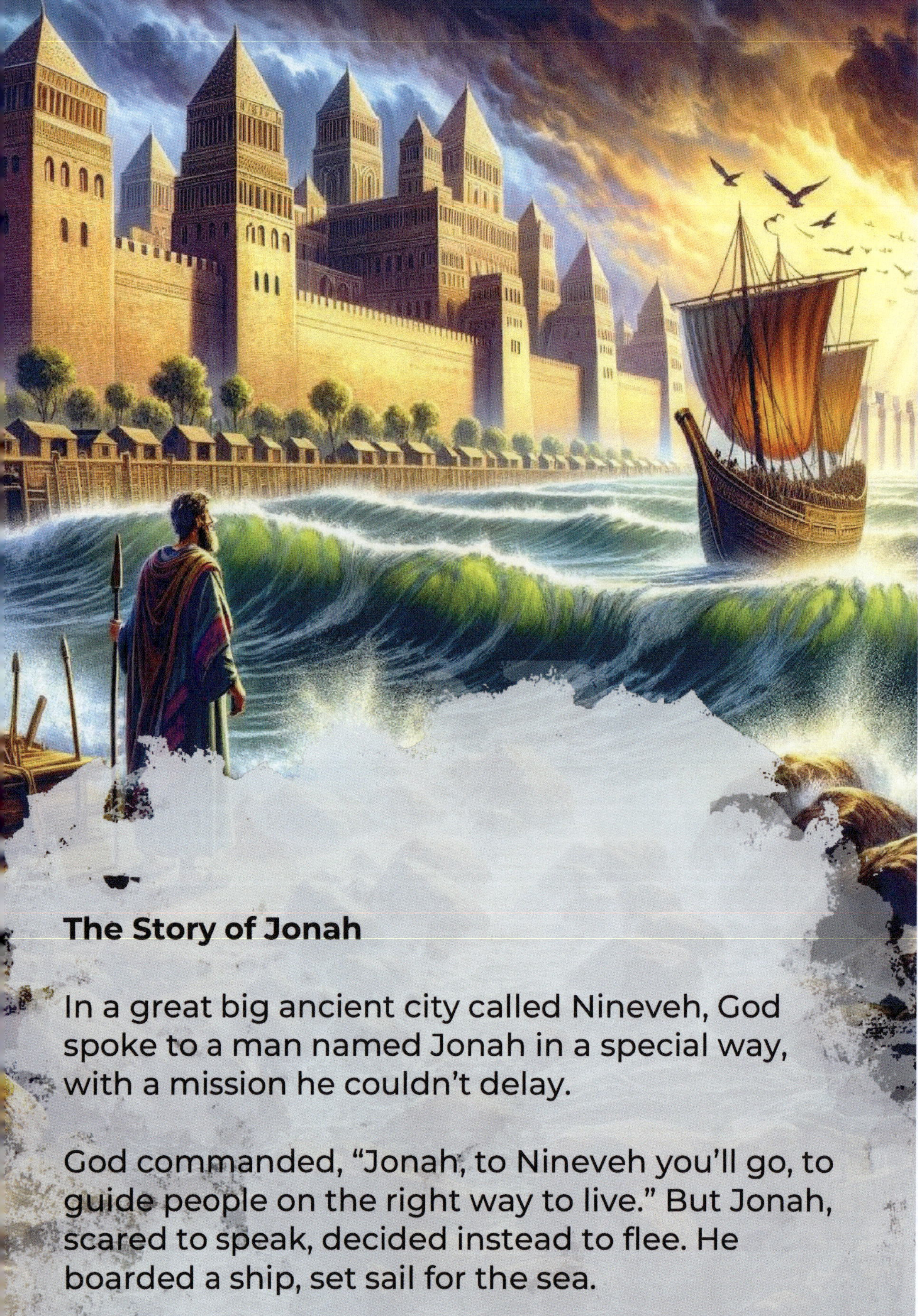

**The Story of Jonah**

In a great big ancient city called Nineveh, God spoke to a man named Jonah in a special way, with a mission he couldn't delay.

God commanded, "Jonah, to Nineveh you'll go, to guide people on the right way to live." But Jonah, scared to speak, decided instead to flee. He boarded a ship, set sail for the sea.

Out on the sea, a storm did roar. Big waves tossed the ship, rocking it to the core. Jonah, on board, in a rebellious mood, didn't listen to God, which was rather rude.

Into the sea, Jonah was thrown. Down he went, deep below. Suddenly, he was swallowed by a fish; there he had to stay, in the belly of the fish. For three long days and nights, he prayed.

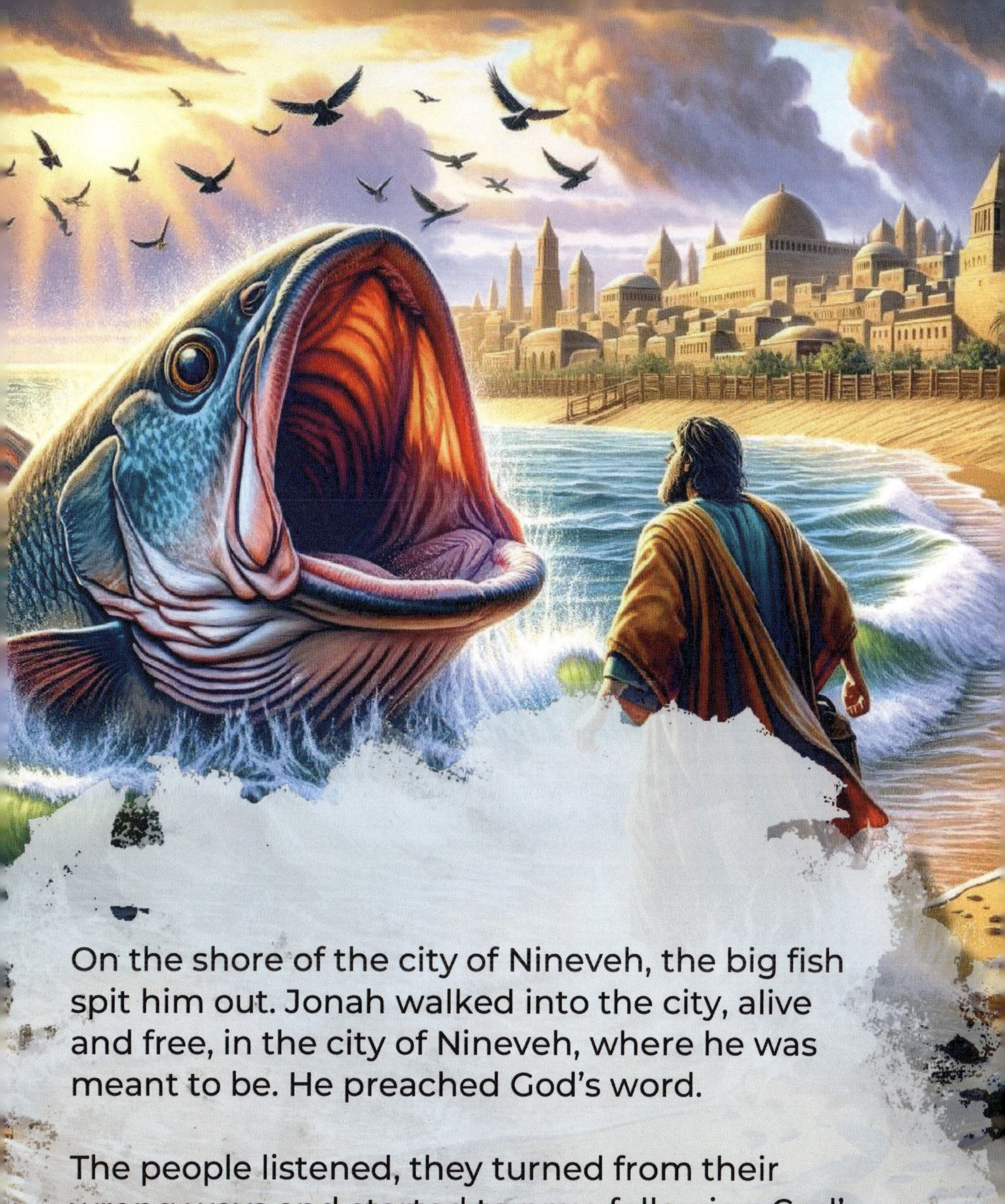

On the shore of the city of Nineveh, the big fish spit him out. Jonah walked into the city, alive and free, in the city of Nineveh, where he was meant to be. He preached God's word.

The people listened, they turned from their wrong ways and started to pray, following God's path, they lived the right way.

**Jonah's story teaches that God has a plan and a way for getting things done. When you listen and trust, God's loving plan will bless you and those around you.**

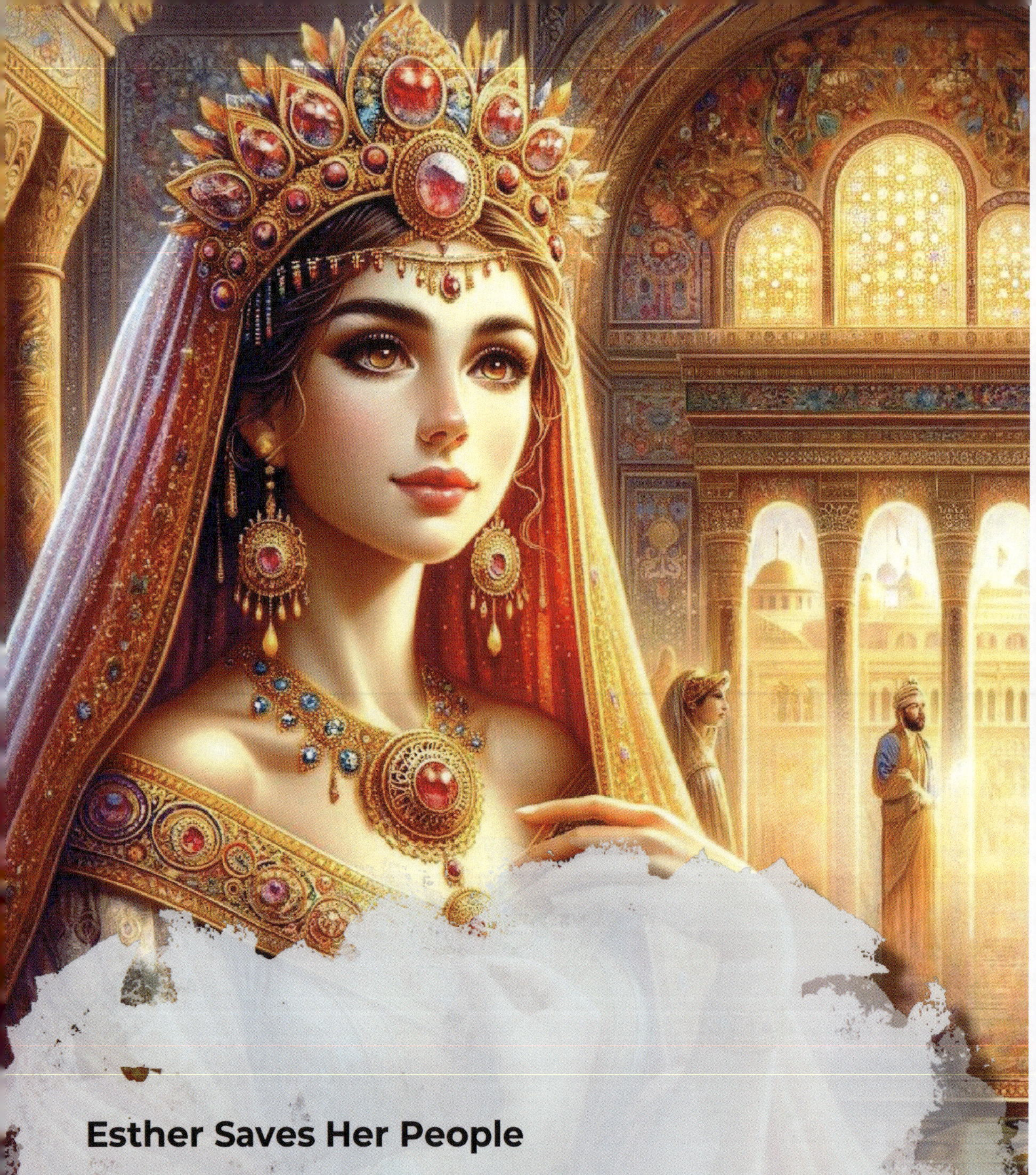

**Esther Saves Her People**

In the ancient Persian Kingdom of Susa, lived a beautiful queen named Esther. Her heart was pure and kind. Both inside and out, she shimmered with radiant beauty.

She was married to King Xerxes, the king of the Persian Empire.

Lurking in the kingdom's court was Haman, a wicked man with a sinister plan to harm God's people.

Esther's cousin Mordecai told her the news of Haman's evil plan.

Esther knew God's help was near. She prayed, "Save my people, Lord, I trust in you."

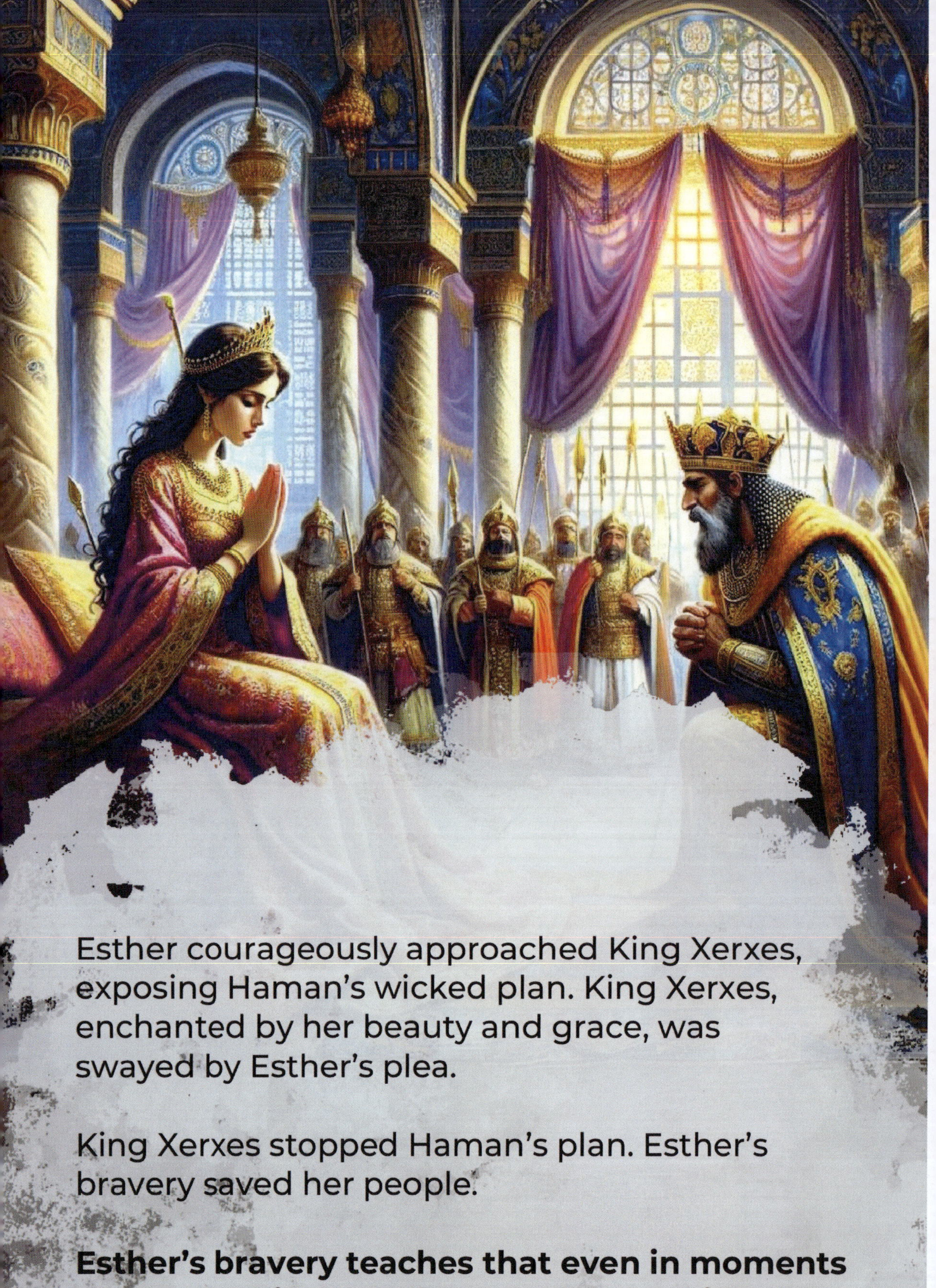

Esther courageously approached King Xerxes, exposing Haman's wicked plan. King Xerxes, enchanted by her beauty and grace, was swayed by Esther's plea.

King Xerxes stopped Haman's plan. Esther's bravery saved her people.

**Esther's bravery teaches that even in moments of fear, seeking help from God and taking the right actions can lead to positive outcomes.**

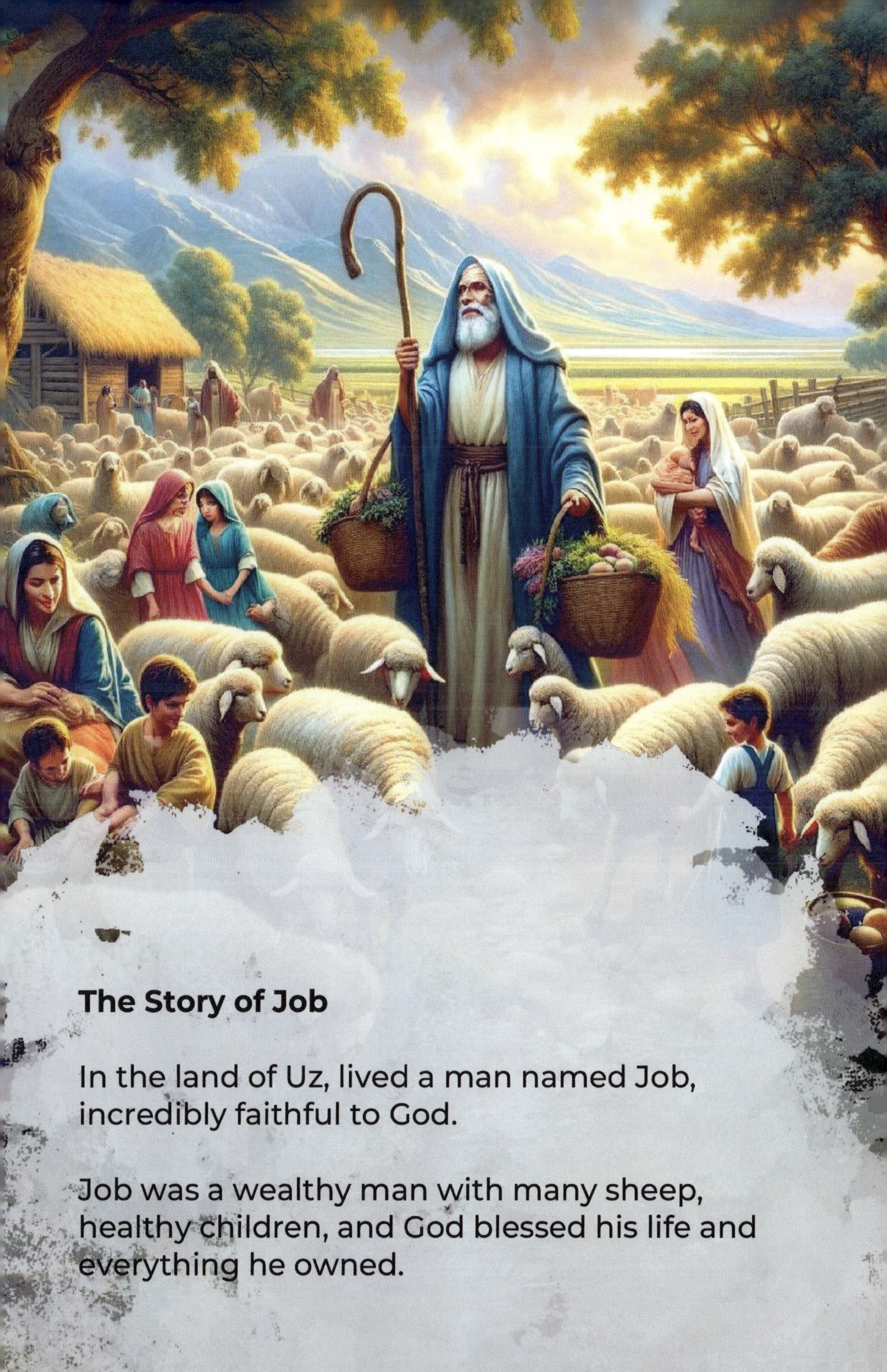

## The Story of Job

In the land of Uz, lived a man named Job, incredibly faithful to God.

Job was a wealthy man with many sheep, healthy children, and God blessed his life and everything he owned.

One day, Satan approached God, “Take away his blessings, let’s test his faith. Job is only faithful because of all his blessings.”

Job lost everything day by day—his wealth, his children—but his faith in God didn't stop.

Boils grew on his skin, pain and suffering, still, Job's faith in God didn't stop.

His friends mocked him, his wife told him to let God go, "Curse God, so your pain can end." Not a word from God, but Job kept his faith.

As Job's health declined, God finally spoke to Job, "Trust in me, I'm wiser than you."

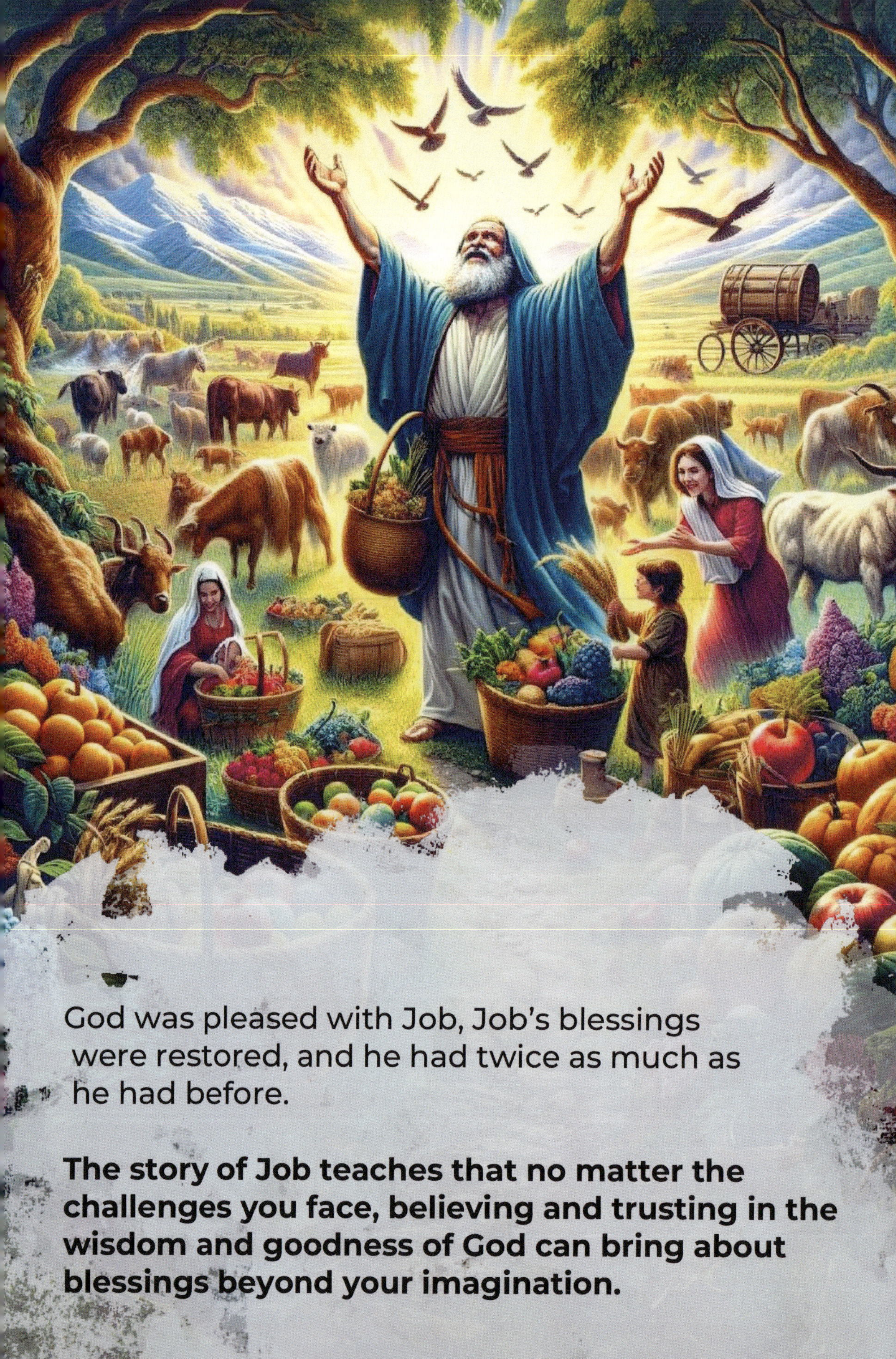

God was pleased with Job, Job's blessings were restored, and he had twice as much as he had before.

**The story of Job teaches that no matter the challenges you face, believing and trusting in the wisdom and goodness of God can bring about blessings beyond your imagination.**

**Elijah and the Ravens**

In the ancient land of Israel, lived a prophet named Elijah, full of faith in God.

In a time of drought, when the land of Israel was dry, no cloud dared to dance, and no rain came from the sky.

In the wilderness, Elijah, in prayer, asked for water and bread. God replied, “You can drink fresh water from the brook.”

Suddenly, with a flutter, a raven came into sight. “I’ve ordered the ravens to feed you,” God said.

Elijah was grateful, ravens brought him his meals. He drank from the brook, year after year.

**In times of need, when things look bleak, ask God for what you need, let your worries fade away. God can send help in magical ways.**

**The Birth of Jesus**

In the small town of Bethlehem, a baby named Jesus was born, in a humble stable. In a crib of hay lay the precious child.

Mary and Joseph, with hearts full of love, welcomed God's gift from heaven above.

Angels rejoiced, singing in the night. The Savior was born.

Shepherds in fields visited the baby that holy night.

Then, Three Wise Men, guided by a star with radiant light, brought gifts to Jesus, precious and rare.

In a manger, where cattle lay low, Jesus slept—a divine child. The Savior had entered the world, the most exciting birth in history.

**The story of the Birth of Jesus teaches about the humble beginnings of the Savior. Extraordinary things can come from the most ordinary places.**

**The Baptism of Jesus**

By the river Jordan, Jesus stood. John, the baptizer, in awe and grace, witnessed a holy, divine embrace.

Into the water, they both did wade. A sacred moment in history was made.

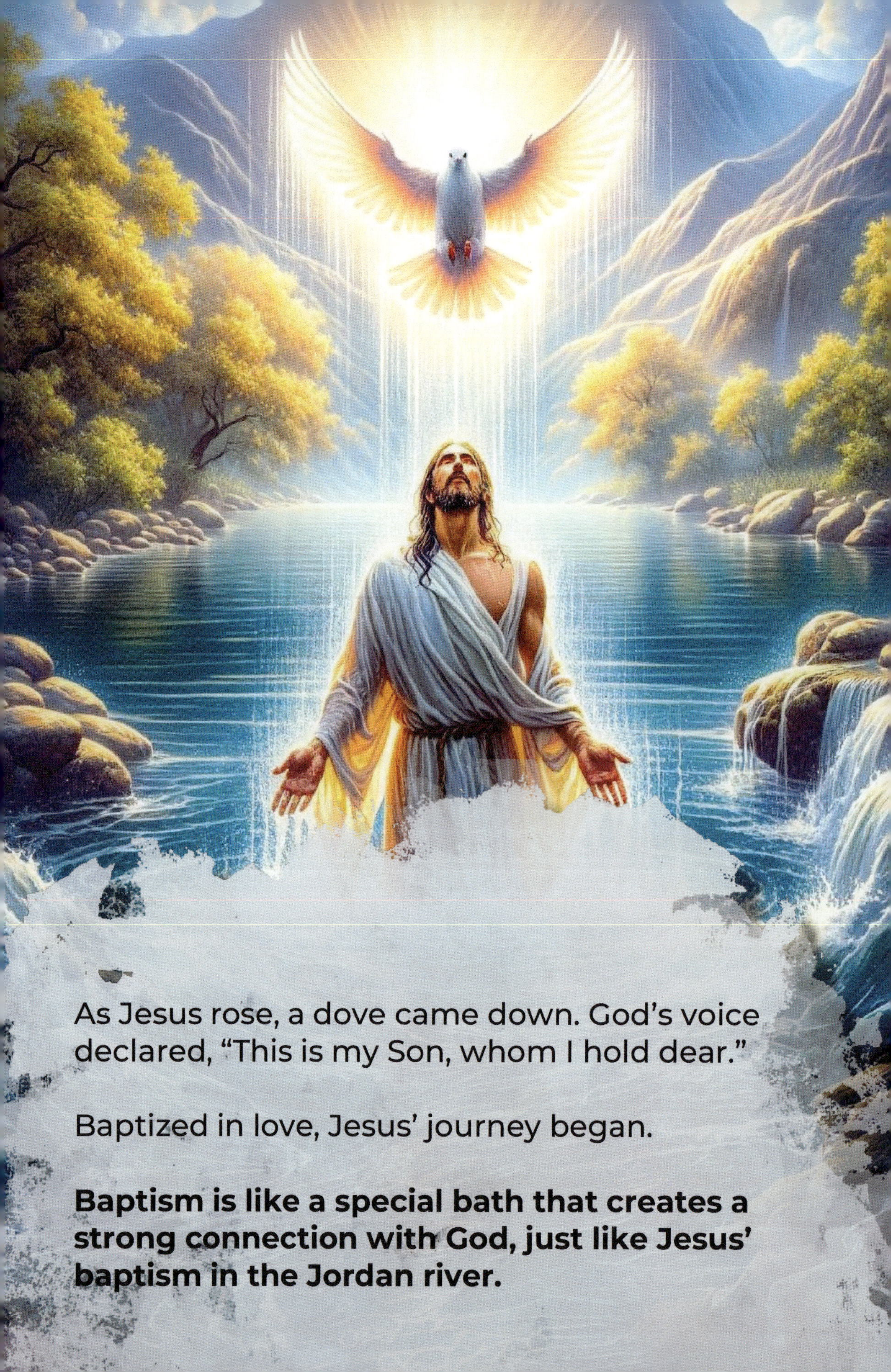

As Jesus rose, a dove came down. God's voice declared, "This is my Son, whom I hold dear."

Baptized in love, Jesus' journey began.

**Baptism is like a special bath that creates a strong connection with God, just like Jesus' baptism in the Jordan river.**

**The Temptation in the Desert**

In the desert's heat, Jesus had tests coming his way.

"Turn stones to bread," Satan said. Jesus stood strong and replied, "Man lives not by bread alone, but by God's Word!"

Then to a mountain, Satan led the way, "See the kingdoms below; they are all for you, bow down to me, and I will give them all to you." Jesus said, "Worship God alone!"

Lastly, to a towering edge, Satan urged, "Jump down, show your power!"

Jesus replied, "Test not the Lord, even though He guards me."

**Jesus teaches to resist breaking God's commands which are meant to protect and bless you.**

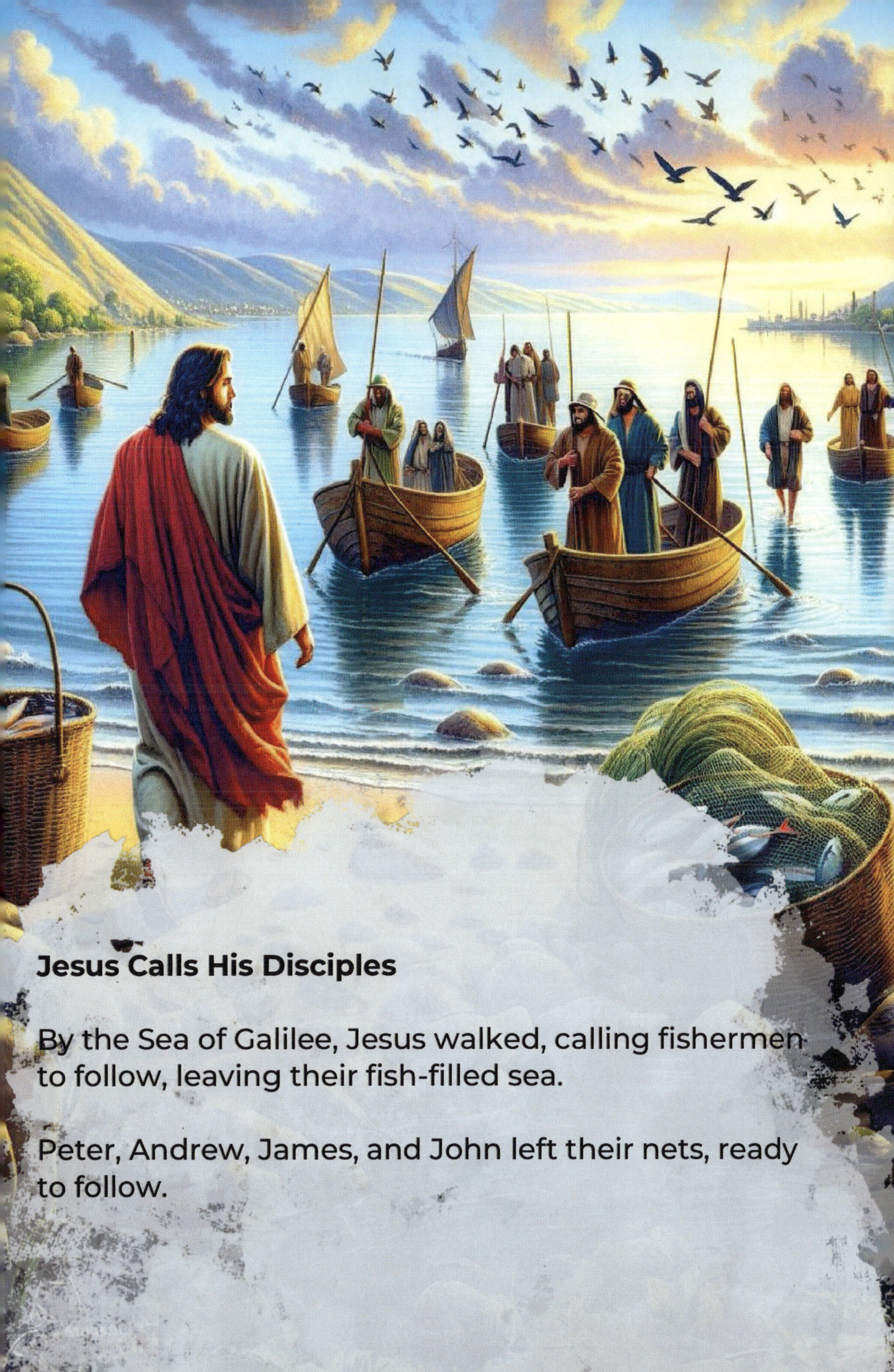

**Jesus Calls His Disciples**

By the Sea of Galilee, Jesus walked, calling fishermen to follow, leaving their fish-filled sea.

Peter, Andrew, James, and John left their nets, ready to follow.

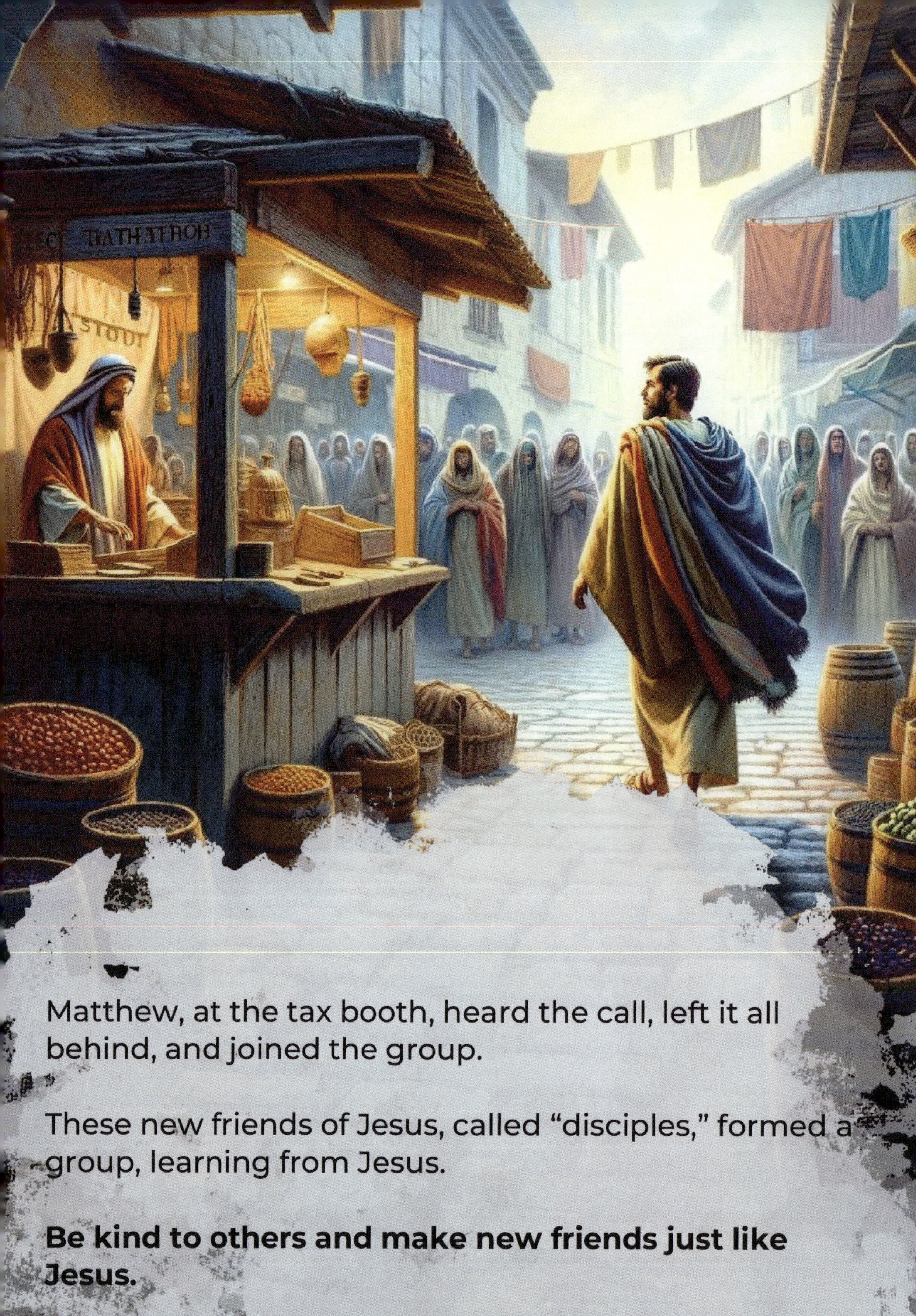

Matthew, at the tax booth, heard the call, left it all behind, and joined the group.

These new friends of Jesus, called “disciples,” formed a group, learning from Jesus.

**Be kind to others and make new friends just like Jesus.**

## The Wedding at Cana

One day, in the town of Cana, there was a wedding feast; guests gathered, and there was joy in the air.

The wine ran dry, and Mary turned to her son Jesus.

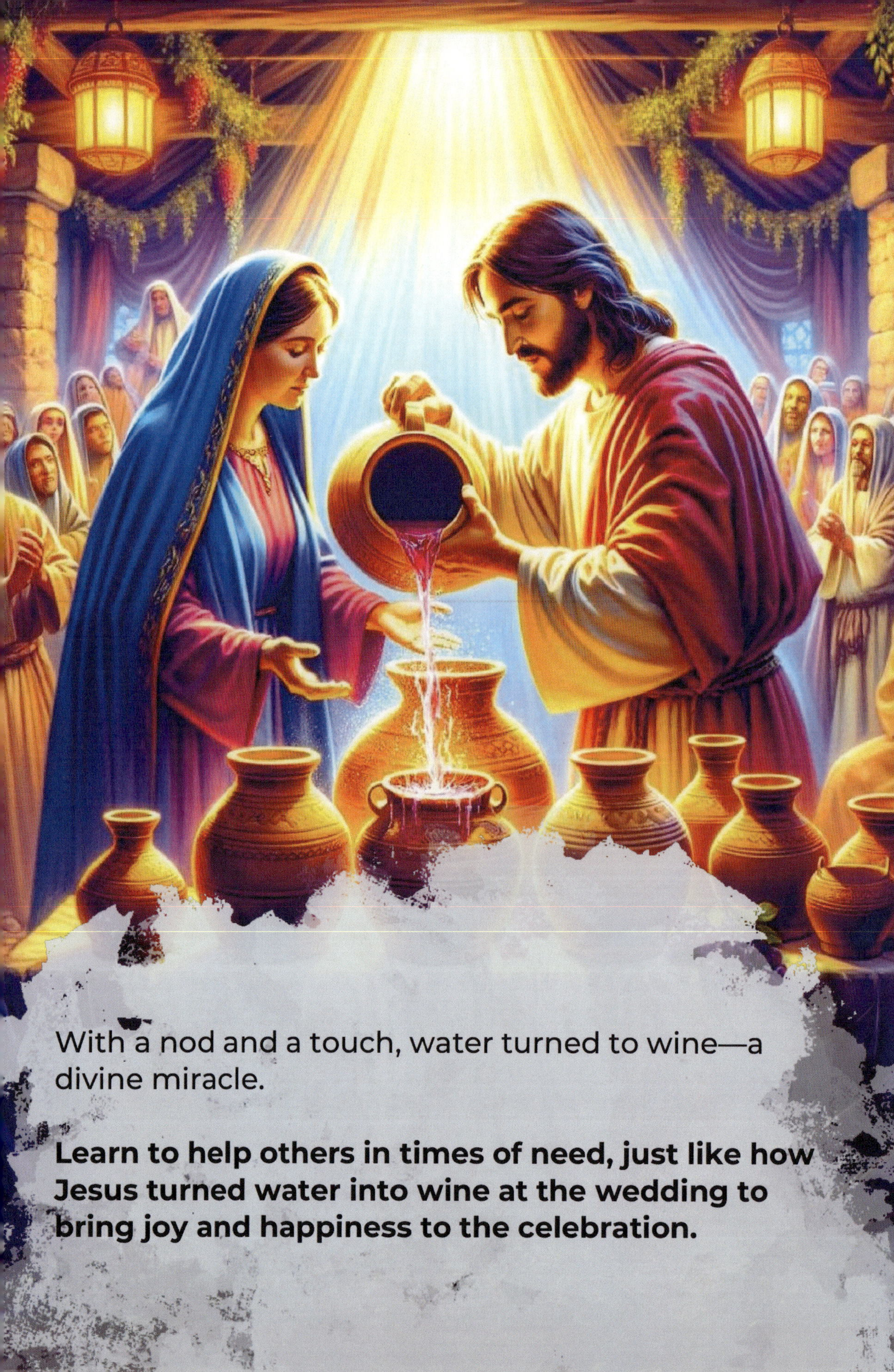

With a nod and a touch, water turned to wine—a divine miracle.

**Learn to help others in times of need, just like how Jesus turned water into wine at the wedding to bring joy and happiness to the celebration.**

**The Feeding of the 5,000**

On a grassy hill, under the bright blue sky, crowds listened for hours as Jesus taught.

The crowds grew hungry, and as night fell, the disciples came to Jesus and asked, "What shall we do?"

With only five loaves and two fish, Jesus prayed and blessed them.

Miraculously multiplied, a feast began, feeding thousands—a part of God's divine plan.

The people marveled at the miracle they saw, a lesson in God's care for His people.

**Just like Jesus turned a little into a lot to feed many, you can share what you have to help others, making a big difference in the lives of those around you.**

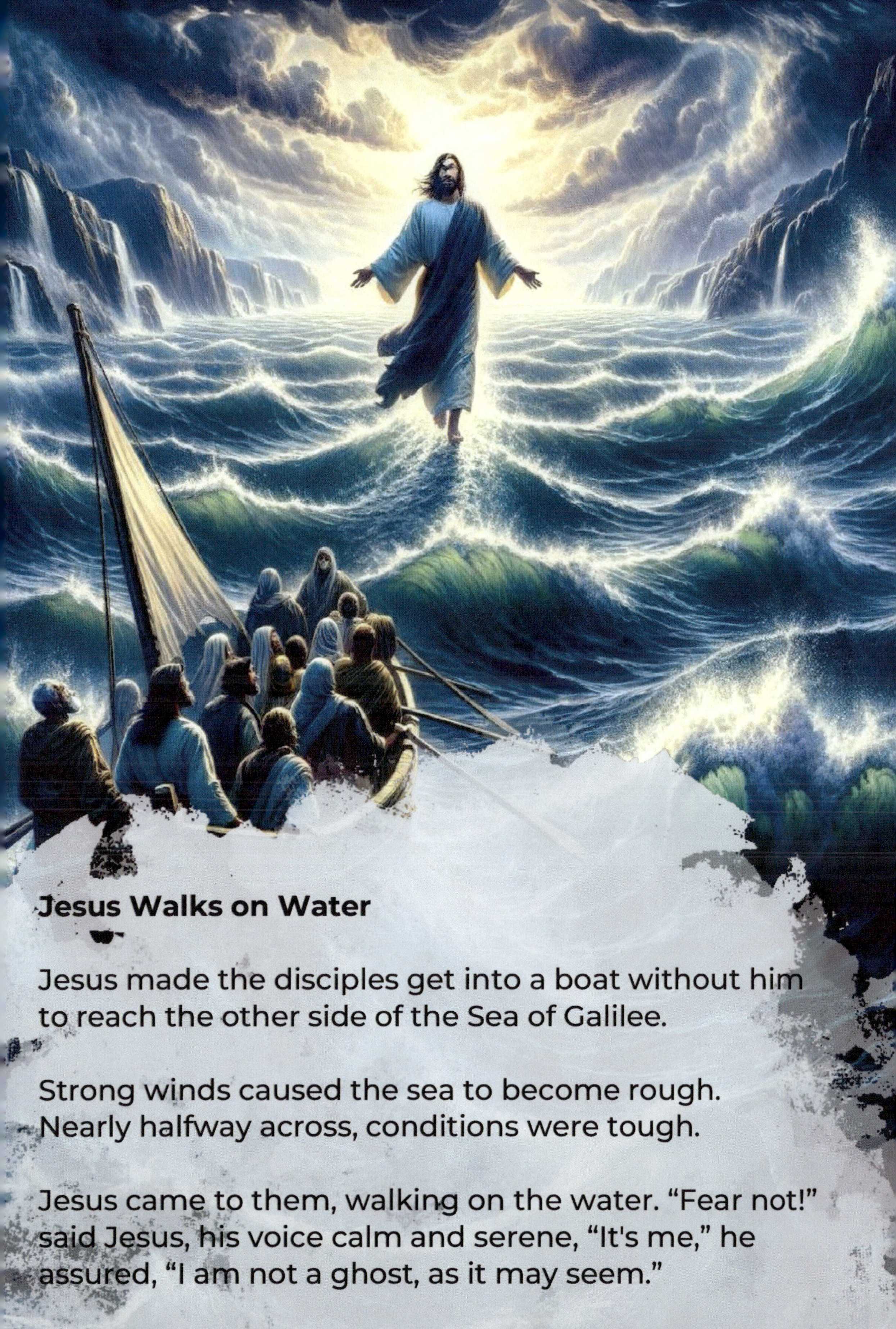

**Jesus Walks on Water**

Jesus made the disciples get into a boat without him to reach the other side of the Sea of Galilee.

Strong winds caused the sea to become rough. Nearly halfway across, conditions were tough.

Jesus came to them, walking on the water. “Fear not!” said Jesus, his voice calm and serene, “It's me,” he assured, “I am not a ghost, as it may seem.”

Jesus invited Peter onto the water. Peter stepped out of the boat, but the wind's force caused him to be scared, and so he began to sink.

"Lord, save me!" Peter cried. Jesus reached out, drawing him near, "You of little faith, why did you doubt?"

As they entered the boat, the wind stopped. The disciples were amazed and said, "Truly, you are the Son of God."

**Just as Jesus helped Peter when he was scared, you can trust in Jesus during tough times, knowing that he is more powerful than you and is always there to help and keep you safe.**

## The Sermon on the Mount

Upon a hill near the Sea of Galilee, Jesus sat to teach. A multitude gathered, eager to learn words of wisdom, pure and true.

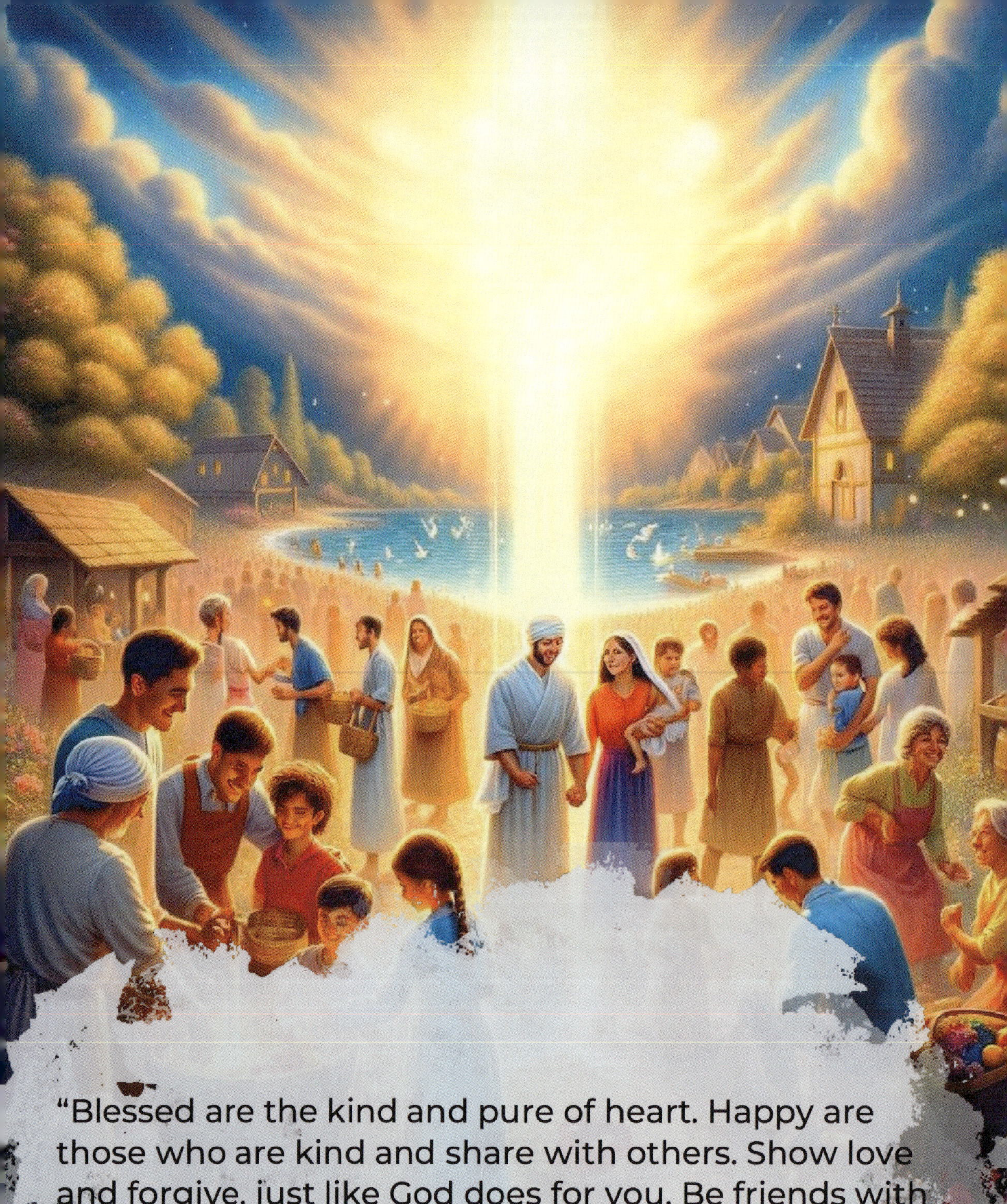

"Blessed are the kind and pure of heart. Happy are those who are kind and share with others. Show love and forgive, just like God does for you. Be friends with everyone and help others. Even if some people aren't nice, be good to them."

**The more you take the time to learn, the smarter and more successful you can live.**

**The Parable of the Good Samaritan**

On a dusty dirt road, a traveler was in need. He was hurt and lonely.

Two walked by, with hearts so cold, ignored his hurt and passed him by.

A Samaritan stopped to help, bandaged his wounds, and showed him care—a perfect example for all to follow.

"Love your neighbor," Jesus taught. Like the Samaritan, spread kindness and love.

**Learn from the Good Samaritan to always be kind and help those in need, showing love to everyone around you.**

**Jesus and the Children**

Children gathered around, laughter in the air. Jesus welcomed them with a gentle hand.

His disciples tried to shoo them away. “Don't keep them away from me,” Jesus declared, “The Kingdom of God belongs to them.”

In His arms, a child He held, a lesson of love.

"Be like children," Jesus said, pure and trusting, free from deceit.

**Jesus teaches to be like children—loving, trusting, and free from deceit—showing that in God's eyes, children are special and lead the way in the book of life.**

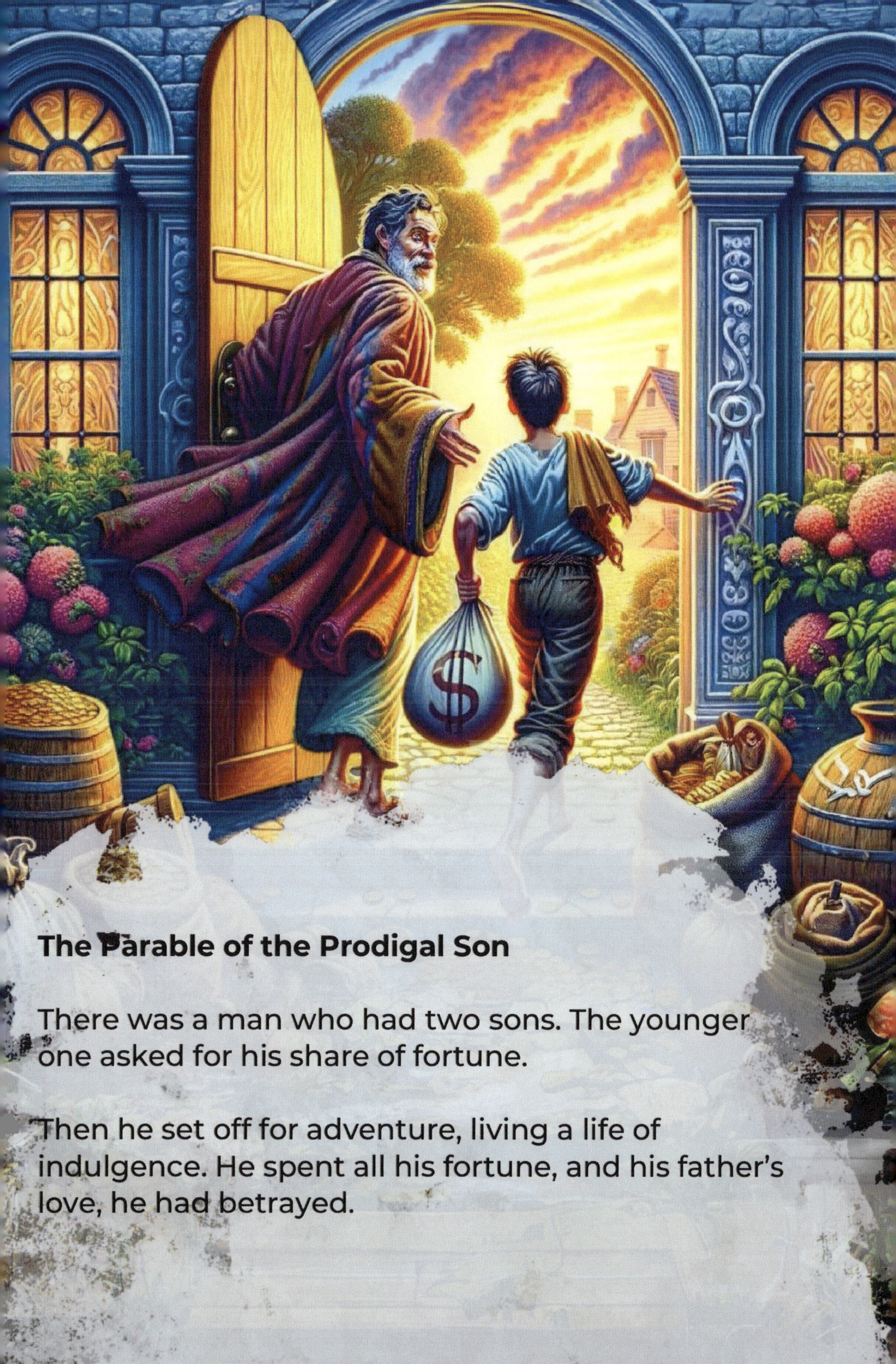

**The Parable of the Prodigal Son**

There was a man who had two sons. The younger one asked for his share of fortune.

Then he set off for adventure, living a life of indulgence. He spent all his fortune, and his father's love, he had betrayed.

Hungry and humble, he came back home, with his head held low.

His father ran to embrace him, told his servant, “Put clothes on him and let’s celebrate. For this son of mine was dead and is now alive again, he was lost and now he is found!”

The father kissed and hugged his son, tears flowing. Years gone by, yet this son was never forgotten, always loved, and completely forgiven.

**Your parents and God will always love you and will forgive you, no matter what, if you come back to them with a humble heart.**

**Jesus Washes His Disciples' Feet**

In an upper room, disciples gathered. Jesus took a dish and water, ready to serve.

Their Lord bowed down low to wash their dirty feet, and the disciples were puzzled, wondering why.

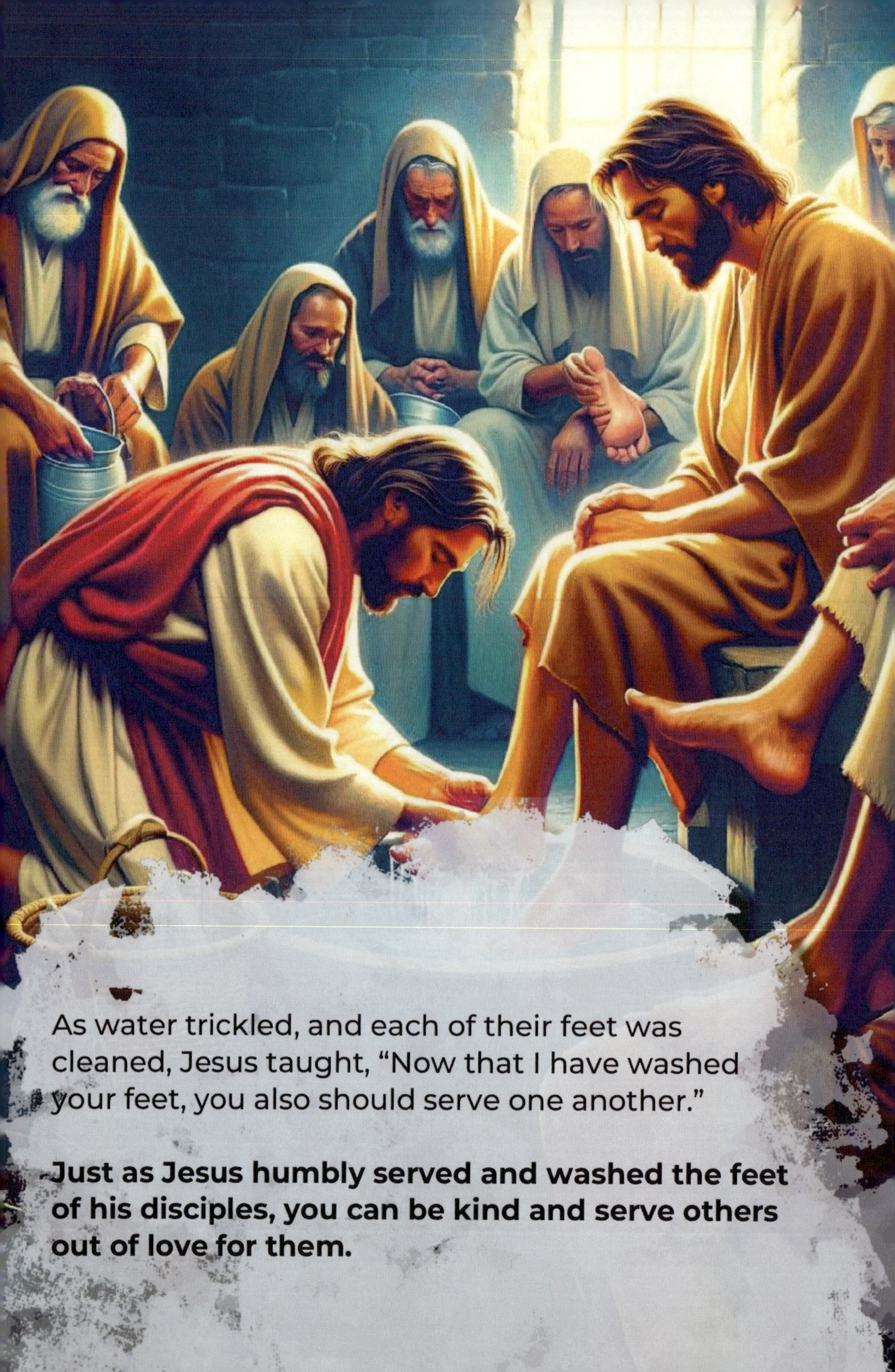

As water trickled, and each of their feet was cleaned, Jesus taught, "Now that I have washed your feet, you also should serve one another."

**Just as Jesus humbly served and washed the feet of his disciples, you can be kind and serve others out of love for them.**

## The Healing of the Blind Man

Jesus and his disciples came to Bethsaida, a town in Galilee. Some people brought a blind man to him.

No light in his eyes, his world black; the man had only known darkness from birth.

With a gentle touch, Jesus restored his sight.

The man was filled with gratitude; he could finally see the colors and beauty of the world.

**Being kind and helping others, like Jesus did for the blind man, brings light and beauty into the world of those you help.**

**The Last Supper**

Jesus with his twelve gathered for a very special last meal.

As they ate, Jesus shared a solemn word, “One of you will betray me.”

Greatly distressed, each one asked, “Am I the one?” Jesus replied, “It is one of you twelve, eating by my side.”

Bread in hand, blessed and broken, Jesus said, “Take, eat; this is my body.”

A cup of wine in hand, after giving thanks, Jesus gave it to them, “Drink, all of you, for this is my blood, poured out for the forgiveness of sins.”

Jesus commands, “Do this in memory of me. Use the bread and wine as symbols of my body and blood.”

**In the story of The Last Supper, Jesus shared a special meal with his friends. Catholics, in worship, remember this sacred night by sharing bread and wine, just like Jesus did, to remind us of his love and sacrifice for all.**

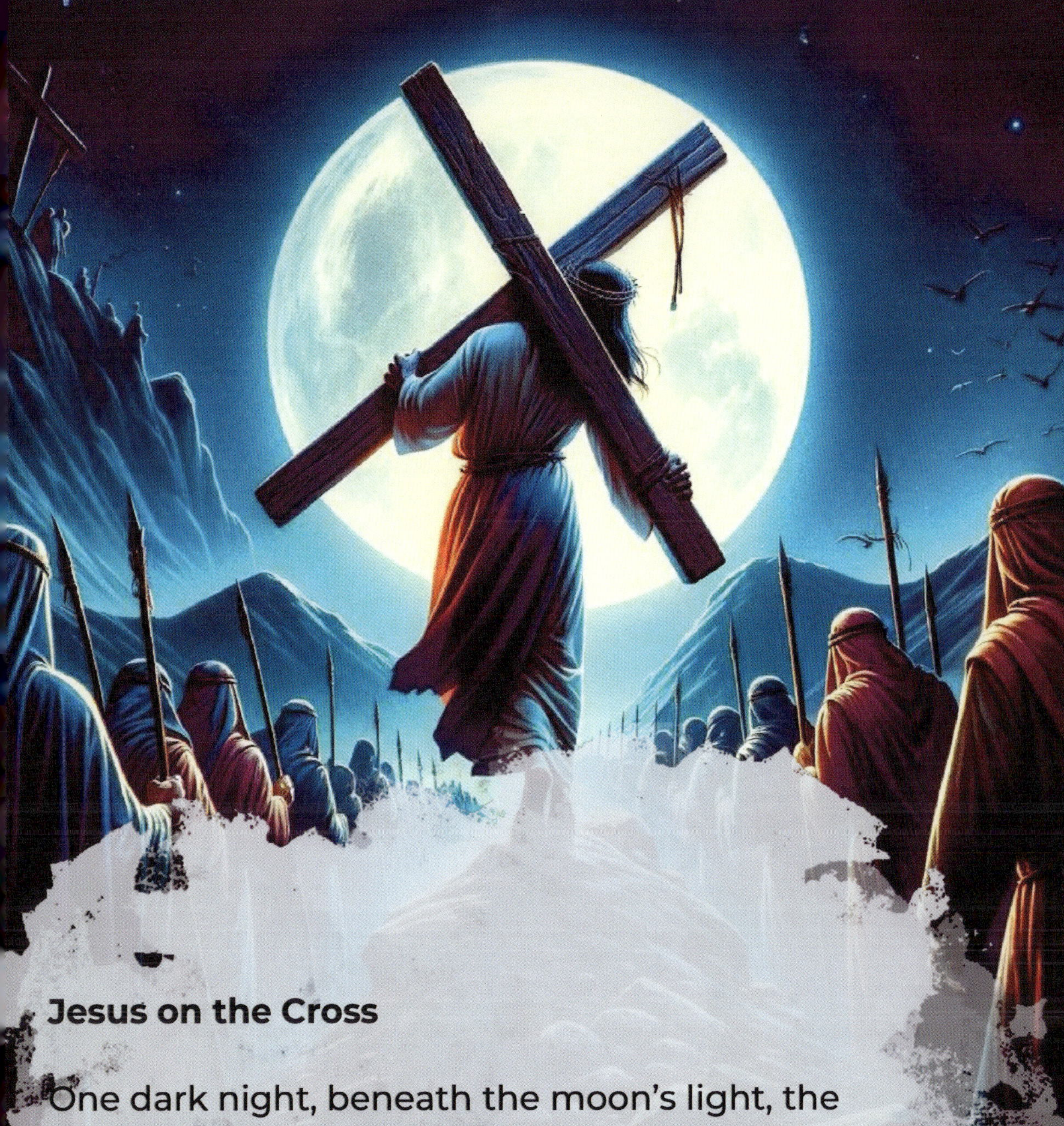

## Jesus on the Cross

One dark night, beneath the moon's light, the disciple Judas Iscariot brought men to arrest Jesus, identifying him with a kiss, calling him "master," giving him away.

Jesus was arrested, led on a walk up a hill, carrying a heavy wooden cross on his back.

Jesus was punished for our sins, nailed to the wood, arms stretched wide.

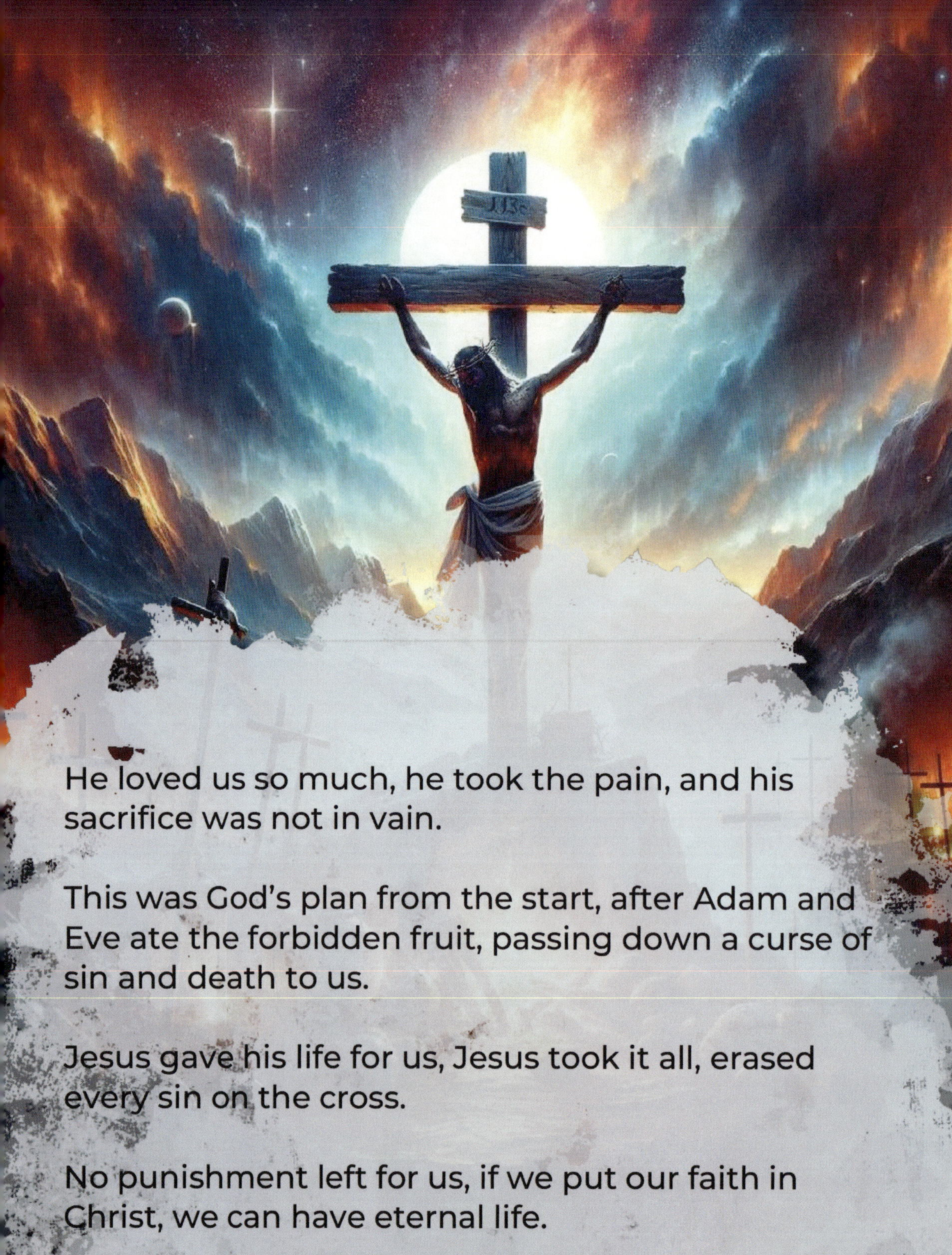

He loved us so much, he took the pain, and his sacrifice was not in vain.

This was God's plan from the start, after Adam and Eve ate the forbidden fruit, passing down a curse of sin and death to us.

Jesus gave his life for us, Jesus took it all, erased every sin on the cross.

No punishment left for us, if we put our faith in Christ, we can have eternal life.

**In the story of Jesus on the cross, we learn about the incredible love he had for everyone. Jesus took away our sins and promises eternal life to those who believe in him.**

**The Empty Tomb**

On the third day after Jesus died, God did something amazing; He raised him back to life.

Early one morning, Mary Magdalene, a friend of Jesus, went to visit the tomb where Jesus was buried.

To her surprise, the entrance was open wide; the stone had been rolled away. Jesus was not there.

There, on the rolled-away stone, sat an angel of God. His appearance was like lightning, his clothing white as snow.

The angel said, “Do not be afraid, Jesus is not here, He’s alive! He has risen!”

**The story of Jesus rising from the dead teaches that God’s love is so powerful that it can conquer even death.**

## Jesus Appears to Mary Magdalene

As Mary stood outside the tomb, tears in her eyes, two angels appeared, dressed in dazzling white. "Why are you crying?" they asked.

"They have taken Jesus away," she replied.

Just then, Jesus stood right before her very eyes. "Go and tell the disciples, I am alive!"

Mary Magdalene ran to the disciples with the news, "I have seen the Lord!"

**Just like Mary saw Jesus again after thinking he was gone, we can trust that God's love brings happiness and good news, even when we're feeling sad.**

**The Road to Emmaus**

Two friends set out, walking toward a village. From Jerusalem to Emmaus, they chatted along the way.

A stranger joined them, “Why are you so sad?” he asked, a twinkle in his eye. The friends poured out their hearts, talking about Jesus, a wonderful man they knew. But now that He was gone, their hearts felt blue.

The stranger began to explain how in the ancient Scriptures, Moses, Prophets, every page, told the tale of love. Jesus, the Savior, was always near.

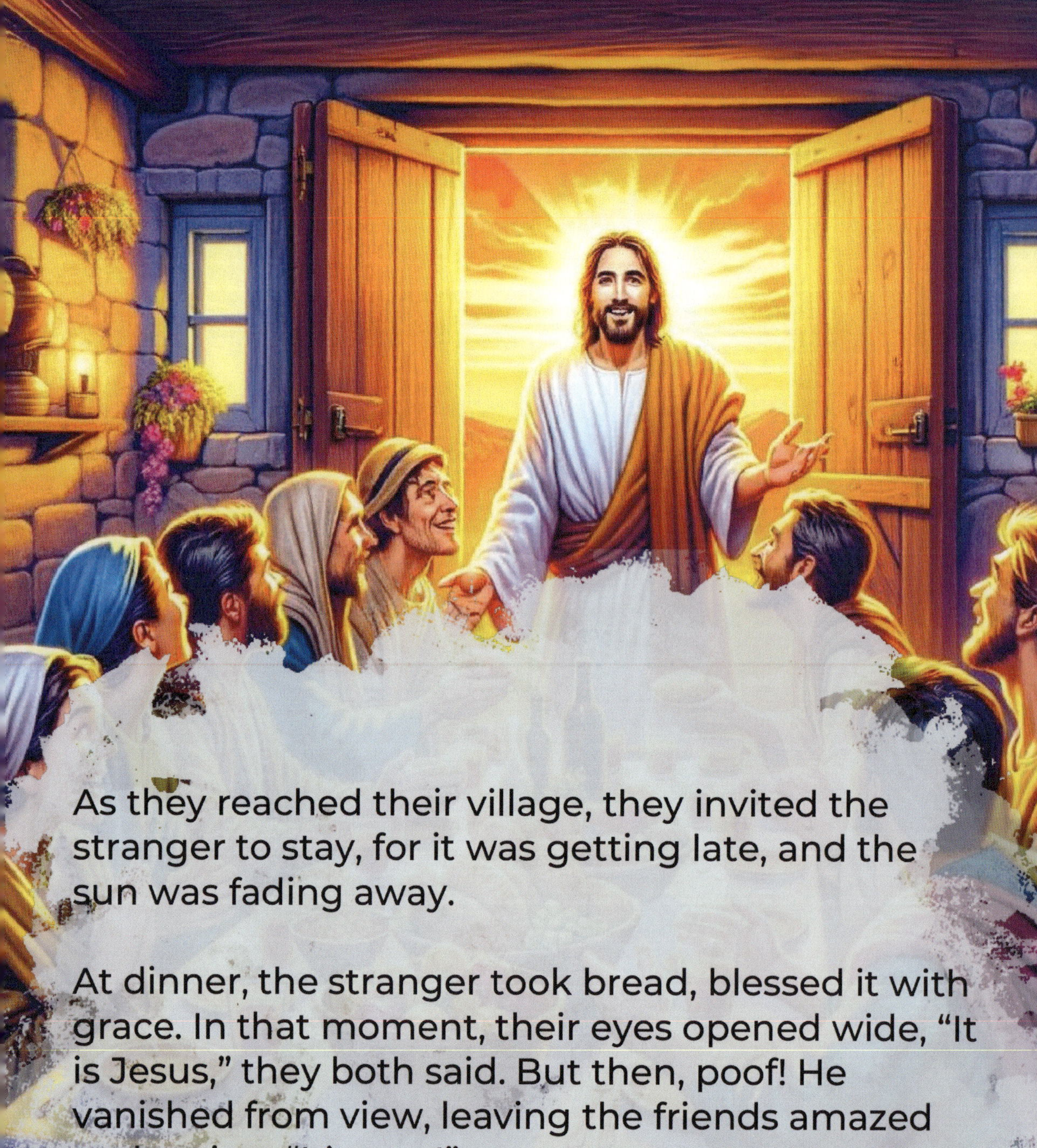

As they reached their village, they invited the stranger to stay, for it was getting late, and the sun was fading away.

At dinner, the stranger took bread, blessed it with grace. In that moment, their eyes opened wide, "It is Jesus," they both said. But then, poof! He vanished from view, leaving the friends amazed and saying, "It's true!"

Filled with joy, they rushed to share the news about Jesus being there.

**The story teaches us that even when we feel sad or lonely, Jesus is always with us, just like he was with the friends on the road to Emmaus.**

## The Ascension of Jesus

After Jesus was raised, He kept appearing to His disciples for 40 days. On the 40th day, Jesus led his disciples to the village of Bethany. There, Jesus began to ascend, rising from the ground and disappearing into the clouds. The disciples watched in wonder and awe, straining their eyes, trying to catch their last look.

Two angels appeared, saying, “Jesus will be back; have no fear! In the same way as you saw him leave.”

**This story shows us that even though you can’t see Jesus, he is always with you, watching over you. Just like the disciples watched Jesus ascend into the clouds, we can have faith that one day he will come back**